P9-BVH-130

3RD EDITION

Foundation Guide *for* Religious Grant Seekers

Francis J. Butler & Catherine E. Farrell
Co-Editors

SCHOLARS PRESS
Atlanta, Georgia

SCHOLARS PRESS
HANDBOOK SERIES

FOUNDATION GUIDE FOR
RELIGIOUS GRANT SEEKERS
Francis J. Butler & Catherine E. Farrell
Co-Editors

Table of Contents

75935

Foundation Guide for Religious Grant Seekers
THIRD EDITION

Library of Congress Cataloging in Publication Data

Butler, Francis J.
  Foundation guide for religious grant seekers.

  (Scholars Press handbook series)
    1. Church finance--Handbooks, manuals, etc.
    2. Church charities--Handbooks, manuals, etc.
    3. Endowments--United States--Directories.
  I. Farrell, Catherine E. II. Title. III. Series.
  BV774.5.B87 1987   262'.0068'1   87-9467
  ISBN 1-55540-121-X

Acknowledgements

The Third Edition of the Foundation Guide for Religious Grantseekers was made possible through a grant provided by the Lilly Endowment. The Endowment, which has been an influential force in the enhancement of religious life in contemporary America, was instrumental in assisting FADICA in the preparation of the first two editions of the Guide. The editors are grateful to the Endowment and in particular Dr. Robert Lynn for his encouragement in the updating of this publication.

Research for this current edition was undertaken with the help of the Foundation Center. The editors wish to express their sincere appreciation to Margot Brinkley, Director of the Washington, D.C., office of the Center, and to her staff who facilitated FADICA's efforts to produce the third edition.

Finally, the meticulous and thorough work of the chief researcher of the project, Catherine E. Farrell, is to be acknowledged and warmly praised. Through Catherine Farrell's conscientious work the publishers are able to provide an excellent resource to lighten the task for the religious grant-seeker.

Introduction

Although religion, as a category of "charitable" activity, accounts for nearly one-half of all private philanthropy in the United States, there are relatively few foundations active in the field of religion. The fact that private foundations with a genuine interest in religion are few and far between has made it difficult for religious organizations to know where to turn for help from foundations.

There has long been a need for a practical guide to help religious organizations (Catholic, Protestant and Jewish) locate foundations that might likely fund their projects or programs. With the exception of de Bettencourt's *The Catholic Guide to Foundations*, (Washington, D.C.: Guide Publishers, 1973), there has been no guide devoted solely to religious grant seeking until this one, which was first published in 1979. This third edition represents a number of changes and improvements over its predecessor issued in 1983.

This, however, is not a "directory" of foundations interested in religion. A directory implies a comprehensive listing of foundations with detailed information about each. While this book does contain some minimal information about 407 foundations with a history of religious grant making, its basic function is to guide the reader to the right sources of information about these and other foundations so that he/she can undertake the necessary research to identify which ones, if any, would be interested in his/her proposal. The targeted approach is preferable (and more effective) in grant seeking than is the scattered approach. Too much precious time, money, and good will are lost through the indiscriminate barrage of proposals to foundations about which little or no research has been done. The chances of obtaining a grant improve in proportion to the research effort made to pinpoint those foundations with interests and priorities corresponding to the grant seeker's.

There is no way except through careful research to know which of the 23,600 grant-making foundations in the nation would be willing to fund a particular project. Foundations do not keep a list of grants available for the upcoming year. Instead, most foundations make broad statements of purpose such as "to aid social, educational, charitable, religious, or other organizations serving the common welfare." Proposals from grant seekers are considered at board meetings of the foundations and funding decisions are made. Time should be taken to investigate thoroughly the foundations to which proposals are sent. An important point in grant searching is the assurance that the foundation is interested in a specific field of endeavor. This guide will enable seekers to locate compatible foundations.

This book also intends to help answer the question: Is a foundation grant really what is needed or wanted? Not only is a foundation grant hard to get but it can, in some cases, be counter-productive. What may be needed might not be foundation support, but better support from an organization's own constituency since its long-term financial well being lies there, not with foundations. To the extent that the prospect of foundation support distracts one from that realization, genuine harm is done.

Finally, the guide may help an applicant realize that foundations have a rather limited place and role in private philanthropy in general and in religious philanthropy in particular. The guide, therefore, presents a four-point plan to aid in building one's own constituency.

Section I

SOURCES OF INFORMATION AVAILABLE ON FOUNDATIONS

The Foundation Center

The Foundation Center is the only nonprofit organization which exists solely to gather, analyze, and disseminate information on American private foundations and their grants. It was established by foundations to provide information for the grant-seeking public and is largely maintained by contributions from foundations. The Center provides (1) free library service to the walk-in public and (2) invaluable publications with information on philanthropic giving and how to determine where to apply most appropriately for funding. (See below for description of these publications.) The Center operates libraries in New York, Washington, Cleveland, and San Francisco. In addition, it supplies publications and other resources to cooperating collections in over 150 public, university, government, and foundation libraries in 50 states, Mexico, and Puerto Rico. (See *Appendix A* for locations of these libraries.) The Center provides the following services at its national collections:

- Reference librarians to help visitors use resource materials
- Free weekly orientations; call for reservations
- Special orientations arranged for groups, classes, or meetings
- Microform and paper copying facilities
- Associates Program—fee service for those needing frequent and immediate access to foundation information.

The cooperating libraries throughout the nation house regional collections. They contain all of the Center's reference works, recent books, and information on foundations, foundation annual reports, and IRS returns pertinent to those foundations within their state or region. Many have staff members who will assist the grant seeker not only in using the local resources but also in contacting the Center's national libraries for more detailed information.

The Publications of the Foundation Center

Copies of the Center's publications are available for free reference use in all of the libraries, and some may be available in other local, public, and university libraries. The following publications may be purchased by writing the Center.

(1) Directories Describing Foundations

Foundation Directory. Includes entries arranged alphabetically within states for approximately 4,400 of the largest foundations. Contains most of the following information: name, address, statement of purpose and interest, officers, financial data, some phone numbers, and some grant application guidelines. (For the latest edition, call Toll Free 800-424-9836).

Source Book Profiles. Annual loose-leaf service with in-depth analyses of programs of 1000 major foundations making annual grants of $400,000 or more per year. The top thousand foundations are profiled on a two-year cycle with 500 new profiles issued per year and over 80 new foundations profiled every other month. Updates are issued when personnel, address, program, etc., changes occur at any foundation profiled to date.

National Data Book. Includes brief entries for over 24,000 foundations. Volume I is arranged alphabetically by name; Volume II contains a complete list of the foundations within each state in descending order of grant amounts. Used together, volumes provide complete address, contact person, and financial information on virtually all active foundations in the United States regardless of size.

Foundation Grants to Individuals. Describes programs of nine hundred and fifty foundations which make grants to individuals. Subject index includes Religion, Religious Studies, Rabbinical Studies, Religious Leadership, and other appropriate subjects for the religious grant seeker.

(2) Indexes to Foundation Grants

Foundation Grants Index. Annual volume which incorporates grants of $5,000 or more of about four hundred and forty foundations.

COMSEARCH Printouts. Computer printouts listing grants and foundations making the grants in particular subject areas (See printout on Broad Topic #12 RELIGION and RELIGIOUS EDUCATION.) Custom computer searches done on more specific topics for foundations and for subscribers to the Center's Associates Program. Searches on The Foundation Grants Index, Foundation Directory.

(3) Guides for Grant Seekers

Foundation Fundamentals, 3rd edition 1986: A guide to funding research.

Internal Revenue Service Form (990-PF)

If a foundation qualifies as private, it is required to file a 990-Private Foundation Form which then becomes available to the public on the

microfiche cards. The following information is found on the forms/cards:
- Name and address of the foundation
- Total assets for the year at market and book value
- Telephone numbers (sometimes just the foundation's accountant)
- Total contributions, gifts, and grants received
- List of the contributions, gifts and grants paid during the year
- Principal officers, directors, and trustees
- Detailed financial information

The list of grants paid is particularly useful to the grant seeker because it contains the recipients and amounts. The IRS forms are invaluable because for many of the smaller foundations they are the only source of detailed information; only the larger foundations publish printed annual reports and qualify for directories. The IRS forms are recorded on microfiche cards and complete sets on every foundation can be obtained at the Foundation Center in New York City and Washington, D.C. or from the Internal Revenue Service. Each regional collection has a full set of these cards for the foundations located in its state or region. By the fall of each year, the file should be largely complete for each preceding year. Staff are available at the Center's libraries to assist you in your research with these IRS forms.

Completed IRS forms also put the foundations' giving patterns in perspective. The grant seeker may find a foundation described in the *Foundation Directory* as being interested in "church support," "religious associations," or "religious purposes," only to find in the IRS form that its support in the religious field was miniscule in comparison to the foundations' funding of other fields of interest.

Annual Reports Published by the Foundations

Only about 500 foundations publish and distribute annual reports which serve to inform the public about their activities. Such publications are generally valuable sources of information, containing lists of grants paid and grants committed to future payment, definitions of program interests, names of officers, and detailed financial statements. For the religious grant seeker, the self-description of the areas of funding interest and the lists of grants paid are useful for pointing out the extent of the foundations's interest in religion.

To find out if a foundation publishes a report, consult the *Foundation Directory*. Most of the foundations that publish annual reports are among the 4,402 major foundations listed in edition 10 of the Directory, and the words "report published annually" at the end of the paragraph describing the purpose and activities of the foundation will indicate which they are.

Another place to find out if a particular foundation publishes an annual report is the *Foundation Center National Data Book* available for use at the Foundation Center's national and regional libraries. This two volume publication previously mentioned as listing over 21,000 currently active grant-making foundations marks with an asterisk those foundations publishing annual reports. Most foundations publishing annual reports print enough copies to fill public requests. The Foundation Center's national and regional libraries also have copies of these reports.

State Directories of Foundations

Approximately forty states have directories listing or describing the foundations within their regional or state boundaries. These guides are important sources of information as many foundations award grants only in their locale. These state directories are available at Foundation Center libraries and at some public and university libraries. See *Appendix B* for a bibliography of state foundation directories.

Other Sources of Information

The Catholic Guide to Foundations. Edition 2 (1973). Francis de Bettencourt, P.O. Box 5849, Washington, DC 20014. Guide Publishers, Washington, DC. An alphabetical list of 336 foundations in 48 states with information derived from IRS reports. Because it is very dated, this guide should be used in conjunction with the other source material, especially the latest edition of the *Foundation Directory*, the IRS 990 returns on microfiche, or the state directories to update the information shown. In many cases, foundations listed have ceased to exist.

Foundation Reporter. Taft Group, 5130 MacArthur Blvd., N.W., Dept. C, Washington, DC 20016. Includes 550 major American foundations, board members described, lists of grants paid, and description of purposes. There are nine regional publications and one national publication, updated annually.

Foundation 500. Douglas M. Lawson Association, 39 East 51st Street, New York, NY 10022. Categorizes 500 largest foundations by general subject areas, amount of giving and giving patterns. (Updated yearly).

Annual Register of Grant Support. Marquis Who's Who, 4300 West 62nd Street, Indianapolis, IN 46206. Updated annually. Lists grant programs supported by foundations, government agencies, corporations, etc. Only directory that covers both public and private funding sources.

Where America's Large Foundations Make Their Grants. Public Service Materials Center, 355 Lexington Avenue, New York, NY 10017. Edited by Joseph Dermer. (Updated yearly).

Catalog of Federal Domestic Assistance. Executive Office of the President (OMB), Washington, DC 20503. For sale by Supt. of Documents, U.S. Government Printing Office, Washington, DC 20402. Marvellously indexed, kept up-to-date by loose-leaf additions throughout the year. (This book is helpful to those religious organizations seeking public funding for educational and/or social service purposes).

COMSEARCH Printouts. Foundation Center (Call Toll Free 800-424-9836). Computer produced subject guides to recent foundation grants. An easy to use listing of grants under 114 categories. (Updated annually).

Section II

THE GRANT SEEKING PROCESS

Now that the resource materials have been identified you may be asking, "But how do I actually begin my search for a foundation that makes grants for religious activities?" The following steps and questions should help you get started.

(1) Use the Foundation Center library system. If you cannot travel to one of the national libraries, check your regional collection. Do not hesitate to ask the staff for help. This alone will help you avoid many problems and wrong turns.

(2) Identify foundations with a *possible* interest in your project by using the list in this guide and the directories and indexes described above.

(3) Research *each* of these foundations for answers to the following questions:

 (a) What is the extent of the foundation's religious funding? Examine the IRS forms or the annual reports for the list of grants paid. Look to see what percentage of grants went to religion. Also check on what type of organizations received grants.

 (b) Does the foundation have geographic limitations on its grant making? Look to see if grants were made only in the foundation's locale or on a national or international basis. It is very important to know if a foundation only funds projects in its region. The directories and annual reports contain this information. As a rule, the likelihood of getting a grant from a foundation diminishes with distance. Therefore, be sure you know all of the possibilities in your locale.

 (c) Does the foundation have financial ability to respond to your request? Check the assets and size of the average grant paid out.

 (d) Does the foundation have any specific limitations or conditions on its grant awarding? Check the guidelines on what type of grants will or will not be made. For example, some foundations will not make grants to individuals, nor will they support building funds. These special limitations will be found in the directories describing the foundations.

 (e) Does the foundation publish procedures by which to apply for a grant? Check the directories and annual reports for any possible deadline for submitting proposals and for the schedule of board meetings.

(4) Once you have done the appropriate research on the foundations you plan to approach, you are ready to make the initial contact. This initial contact can be by either telephone or letter to briefly describe your pro-

gram and needs and to ask if the foundation would be interested in receiving a proposal. If there is interest, ask for information concerning the correct procedure, the time for applying, and the possibility of a personal interview. (Often the most effective way to get a grant is through a person-to-person interview.) Contact should first be made with the appropriate person on the foundation's staff. If there is no staff, find the person who has been designated to be contacted. He/she will likely be an officer or trustee. If there is a staff, do not attempt to approach a trustee without the staff's knowing it. This would be not only poor etiquette, but also a ploy that can easily work to your detriment.

(5) The best guidelines in writing a proposal are the ones the foundation itself may provide you. If no guidelines are provided, it is up to you to state your cause as best you can in a format that seems most appropriate to your situation. Be accurate in what is said and avoid grandiose language. Make it evident that you are aware of what has been and is being done by others relative to the needs or concerns to which your proposal is addressed. Proposal writing is largely a matter of common sense and clear narrative writing. The following are certain basic elements that all proposals ought to contain.

(a) Statements of:
- Nature and purpose of your organization. (By way of introduction.)
- The problem or need.
- What you propose to do about it. (Objectives and methods of action.)
- What makes your proposal or approach distinctive from comparable requests from other institutions.
- The anticipated outcome. (What, when, and ways of measuring success.)
- Who is involved in the program and what are their qualifications. (Only cite credentials pertinent to the effort to be undertaken.)
- Expected grant period. (Have you taken into account the amount of time the foundation will need to make its decision?)
- How the proposed program relates to other institutions and resources pertinent to the need described.
- Endorsements or references. (Any enclosed letters of endorsement ought to illumine the particular qualifications of the persons involved in the program and not deal with extraneous qualities.)

(b) Financial information about:
- The budget and overall financial context of the plan.
- The amount of grant support being requested.
- Other sources of support.
- Provision for on-going support of the program. (Vague assurances are not reassuring.)
- Evidence of tax-exemption.

(c) Summary

The highlights of the prosposal ought to be summarized on one or two pages and put at the beginning along with a letter of transmittal.

Several publications designed to help the proposal writer are available through the Foundation Center and may be obtained by writing the New York office or by visiting one of their libraries.

A final reminder is in order about the importance of thoroughly researching the foundations to which you send proposals. No matter what amount of effort is put into it, your proposal will prove worthless if it is sent to foundations which have no interest in your area of concern.

Section III

THE VIEW FROM THE OTHER SIDE OF THE DESK

Foundations, and organizations which seek grants from them, have a common allegiance: both are members of what is increasingly known as the "third sector"—the world of non-profit, private "voluntary" agencies and organizations. The other two sectors are, of course, business and government. All three provide either goods or services, but with significantly different imperatives and motives. Each is integral to American society and our system of checks and balances.

Three significant characteristics of American society largely account for the existence of the third sector: (1) the American impulse to altruism, voluntary giving of money, time and other private resources to meet the needs of others; (2) our penchant to organize ourselves into private, voluntary efforts in order to apply those resources systematically to social problem solving; and (3) our long tradition of pluralism and cultural diversity. Each of these traits also serves to explain the almost uniquely American phenomenon of private foundations.

Although private foundations fully share in the origin and experience of charitable organizations, in whatever field of endeavor—education, social welfare, the arts and sciences, conservation, religion, etc.—there is still a great deal of misunderstanding about their nature and role particularly on the part of the grant seeker.

It is hard for grant seekers to put themselves into the position of the foundation representative. Part of this difficulty is due to the failure of the foundations themselves. By and large foundations have been reticent about explaining their problems and aspirations to the public, sometimes because of a sense of humility consistent with Scriptural injunctions against the dangers of advertising one's own good deeds. More often, however, foundations are reluctant to be too visible lest their explanations about themselves invite an avalanche of requests.

Perhaps the root of the problem lies even deeper. There is almost unavoidable distance between the grant maker and the grant seeker. From the point of view of the aspiring grantee, the foundation often appears to enjoy ample resources or at least enough money to make "just this one grant." Yet, that is not how it looks from the other side of the desk. The foundation official, whether a trustee or staff member, is apt to be aware of a different kind of abundance, namely, the sheer plenitude of significant opportunities for grant making and the relative scarcity of foundation funds to meet even a fraction of these possibilities. Where one sees abundance the other sees scarcity.

This gap between abundance of opportunities and scarcity of available resources necessarily affects the ways in which even the most affluent foundations go about their work. While foundations react to this pressure in different ways, there are at least two contrasting tendencies in their responses.

1) In view of the scarcity of foundation funds and the consequently increased importance of these resources, many foundations prefer to stay with the "tried and true" causes. If a foundation leans in this direction, then it will be more likely to favor support of already existing institutions and to be willing to provide a subsidy for on-going programs or perhaps for "brick and mortar" needs. The foundation, in effect, takes its place alongside of the individual donor and makes a contribution to maintain or improve the *status quo*. Such a donation seldom represents a risk or causes controversy, except, perhaps, from those who were disappointed that this program subsidy did not go to their organization.

2) The opposing tendency leads to a quite different response. In the judgement of some foundation representatives, the preoccupation of supporting the proven institutions and programs deflects foundations from making their most distinctive contributions. At its best American philanthropy has constituted an early warning system about the problems and possibilities that lie ahead in the future. A good grant has been one that has helped illumine the landscape of tomorrow: the needs of our society, what changes are now necessary to prepare ourselves for them, and what pitfalls to avoid as we move into the future.

Philanthropists who accept this view of foundation grant-making recognize a distinction between the role and capacities foundations can assume in our society and the role the individual donor plays.

All positive change involves risk. Foundations, unlike most donors, are uniquely prepared to assume risks in the interests of society. Their distributable funds can be "invested" in imaginative programs and projects whose chances of success are tentative and whose ability to make a "return" (least of all to the foundation) is not important. In very many such cases foundations represent the only feasible source of financial support. Foundations can also afford to live with an unpopular line of inquiry without having to worry unduly about an anxious public. These institutions can stay with issues long enough to weigh the long-term effects or to seek out alternative solutions because they can, if they will, resist the temptation to join the passing parade of fads and fancies.

Such an exploration of the future is not, of course, without its hazards. Foundations can—and do!—guess wrongly about significant issues. It is all the more important, therefore, that foundations have the freedom to admit their errors and thereby to gain the confidence and support of the community at large by searching out the most important problems of the coming years.

The role of the individual donor in private philanthropy contrasts significantly with that of foundations. It would not be overstating the matter to say that the survival of voluntary organizations depends on the continued altruism of the individual donor and not on foundations. The free will contributions of money and service by individual donors are what most private charitable organizations rely on to close the gap between operating income and actual costs. In short, the indispensable role of the individual donor in private philanthropy is subsidizing charitable institutions. The statistics bear this out.

To begin with there are only about 23,600 private grant-making foundations in the United States, and all but about 3,000 are extremely small (with less than one million dollars each in assets). On the other hand, the number of individual donors is legion, comprising practically the whole of the adult community to some degree. (The word "donor" might be misleading in its connotation since what is being referred to is the small contributor as well as the large).

In 1985, individual donors in the United States provided $66.06 billion, or 82.7 percent, of all private philanthropy.* This figure does not include another $5.18 billion in bequests nor does it include the billions of hours of contributed service time. Corporations and businesses contributed $4.30 billion and foundations another $4.30 billion. Altogether, private philanthropy in the United States totalled $79.84 billion that year, only 5.4 percent of which came from foundations.

In the field of religion, the percentage contrast of total contributions made by foundations versus individuals becomes even more extreme. Less than two percent of the $37.73 billion of private philanthropy that was directed to the field of religion during 1985 came from foundations. Almost without exception, the rest came from individual donors and accounted for nearly half (47.2%) of all private giving to charity of any variety!

What can be inferred from these figures in forming a realistic attitude toward foundations and private philanthropy in general when seeking financial support for religious organizations?

For one thing, we can gain a better sense of realism about the limitations of foundations as sources of financial support to religious organizations. The total amount of funds available to religious activities from foundations is infinitesimal compared to the funds contributed by individuals. There are precious few foundations active in the field of religion. In the course of preparing this guide, the authors were able to identify about 407 such foundations from the approximately 4,000 largest throughout the country, and most of these are local in their giving preferences. Moreover,

---

* All figures are taken from the 1985 Annual Report of the American Association of Fund Raising Counsel, Inc., entitled *Giving USA*.

the volume of requests these foundations typically receive far exceeds their available funds. In general, therefore, the chances of getting a grant from a foundation are slim and become narrower the greater the distance separating the foundation from the organization applying for a grant. It is therefore very important to target one's grant request as precisely as possible through careful research in identifying those foundations most likely to be able and willing to respond positively.

Second, one ought to respect the fact that foundations are a scarce source of risk capital for program areas where change and development are needed and where there is no other source of support. There are few other comparable sources of this "venture capital" available to the voluntary sector. Foundations, therefore, should not be asked to replace the private donor in subsidizing the operating and normal program expenses of charitable organizations, nor to aid projects whose support could come from the organization's own constituency if an adequate effort were only made. Such grants would amount to a misuse of a very limited and valuable resource for both the society and for religion in particular.

Third, it is unwise automatically to look to foundations as a solution to the financial needs or problems of your organization or program. The very existence of foundations—all that free money—engenders in too many charitable and religious organizations a reflexible reaction to turn to them, the foundations, for help. In this connection, it can be parenthetically noted that grant seekers often turn to private foundations without considering the resources available for charitable purposes within grant-making religious bodies. Nearly every major denomination maintains a funding entity of some type. Many of them are significantly larger than the typical private foundation.

The prospect of foundation aid can serve to harm charitable organizations if allowed to distract them from the realization that their long term survival and well-being depends on recieving aid from their own support community. Rarely can foundations be found to be a direct part of the constituency of any one charitable or religious organization. It is a major, and sometimes fatal, error for charities to perceive foundations as such.

The fact that the future of voluntary organizations and institutions depends almost entirely upon the extent to which they are able to develop a strong and lasting financial base from a compassionate support community. This means recognizing potential members of this community, nurturing them, and actively involving them in the life of the organization and its programs. Thus if, in responding to the imperative of raising more funds, you find yourself spending most of your time and energy trying to interest foundations in your program needs and not trying to develop your own support community, you are probably doing everybody, including yourself, a disservice. To better understand how a voluntary organization can develop a lasting financial base, the following section is provided.

Section IV

BUILDING CONSTITUENCY SUPPORT

A voluntary organization is wise to seek a broad base of support. Dependency on a single source of support, no matter how adequate and comfortable it may be for the time being, is almost certain to lead to severe financial problems in the future, probably the near future. Typically, a broad base of support for a volunteer organization would include all or most of the following:

(1) Fees for service, tuition, or membership
(2) Endowment income
(3) Contributions
(4) Revenue from federal, state, or local government agencies
(5) Sale of publications
(6) Auxiliary enterprises (housing and food services)

No matter what percent of the annual budget is derived from contributions, it is desirable to obtain gifts from a variety of sources. Here again, dependency on a single source, or a very small number of donors, places an organization in a high-risk position. Individuals may die, change their interests, or even become disenchanted with the organization. Foundations rarely provide extended funding. Corporations tie their giving to profits which usually fluctuate from year to year, and they generally like to spread their contributions over a rather large number of recipients. In addition, very few foundations or corporations will give to organizations which have a specific religious orientation.

Four Characteristics of Successful Fund Raising

Financial stability for most voluntary organizations requires that the fund raising effort be successful. Succcess means that annual objectives for number of donors and dollars are met. There are four characteristics of successful fund raising which are quite prominent. These will not exist to the same degree with all groups, and a single organization which is successful in fund raising may see some variations in these characteristics from year to year.

(1) Program Worthy of Support

The first characteristic of a successful fund raising effort is that the organization maintains a program of service which is worthy of support. It has a reputation for doing well what it purports to do. Those who know about the organization, if only slightly, believe it is doing something worthwhile. The extent to which an organization is known and truly understood will vary greatly. Some are much more adept than others in publicizing their activities. The point is, when an organization is successful in raising funds, it will be providing a service or program which any fairminded person who came in contact with it would agree to its deserving support.

(2) Constituency with Ability to Provide Support

The second characteristic of a successful fund raising effort is a constituency which has the financial ability to provide the required support. This may be a natural constituency or a developed constituency. Examples of a natural constituency would be alumni of an educational institution, former patients of a hospital, season members of a symphony orchestra, or parishioners of a church. A developed constituency would include individuals, corporations, and organizations which have been made aware of the voluntary organization's program and have shown a willingness to help support it. They may or may not become directly involved with the program or service of the charitable organization.

In attempting to establish a developed constituency, it is important to identify those who truly have the financial potential for providing support. Many organizations tend to look far and wide for prospects, when their best potentials may be within a few blocks or miles of the institution. As a matter of fact, most organizations which are successful in fund raising receive significant gift dollars from board and staff members before seeking outside support.

Regular and systematic approaches need to be made to the constituents to keep them informed. It is hazardous to assume that even those who are fairly close to the work of an organization are fully aware of the program and financial situation. Newsletters, brochures, audio visuals, and on-location visits will help interpret the organization to its natural and developed constituents.

(3) Fund Raising Plan

The third characteristic of an organization which is successful in obtaining gift support is that it has a plan for fund raising. The plan may be a few pages in length or it may be a large and greatly detailed document. Size is not important. What is essential is that the effort be given careful thought and that it represents the commitment of the fund raising staff, the chief executive, the administrative staff, and the board of directors. Some of the elements in a typical fund raising plan will include:

(a) Statement of organizational objectives.
(b) Narrative which justifies gift support.
(c) Detailed financial goal(s).
(d) Time schedule for each phase of the fund raising effort.
(e) Budget for fund raising program.

(f) Decision regarding personal solicitation, telephone solicitation, direct mail, benefit or special event, sale of merchandise.

(g) Determining type of gift sought-outright, gifts with reservation of life income, or bequests.

(h) Decision whether gift principal or income only is to be used.

(i) Establishing method of receiving gifts, gift acknowledgements, gift accounting.

(4) Leadership for Fund Raising

The final characteristic of an effort which is successful in fund raising is that there are leaders who are able to implement the fund raising plan. Most experienced development officers would agree that this is the most important of the four characteristics cited. Why is leadership for fund raising so important? It is rather well accepted that people give to people. The personal relationship that exists between solicitor and donor will usually be the determining factor.

Leadership for fund raising divides into two categories, staff leadership and volunteer leadership. Both are critical if the organization hopes to obtain maximum results. Staff leadership for fund raising begins with the chief executive. This person must give it a high priority even though he may spend a relatively low percent of his time in fund raising. Operating responsibility for fund raising rests with the development officer. This person must coordinate the fund raising activities of the chief executive and other staff members and the volunteer fund raisers. The volunteer leadership for fund raising usually begins with the board of directors. There may also be an advisory board or a development committee which takes primary responsibility.

Whatever the structure, organizations that achieve well in gift support have volunteers who are effective in giving and getting gifts. Conversely, most fund raising failures can be traced to a lack of leadership for fund raising. Experience shows that an organization will be successful in raising funds if it has a program worthy of support, identifies or develops a constituency with ability to give, prepares a plan for fund raising, and then enlists leaders to carry out the plan.

Section V

FOUNDATIONS WITH PAST INTEREST IN FUNDING RELIGIOUS ORGANIZATIONS

The following list of foundations with a history of funding religious activities is not to be considered all-inclusive. It was largely compiled from the most recent IRS returns of each foundation. These were examined in the fall of 1986 to determine the actual extent of its grant making in the field of religion. The principal researcher reviewed the entries in the second edition of the *Foundation Guide* and found by checking the federal returns that one hundred-forty seven changes had to be made to the previous 384 entries of the second edition of the Foundation Guide. The current edition contains information on 407 foundations which meet the following criteria: (1) made grants to more than one religious organization (unless an unusually large amount), (2) total grants to religion were either $25,000 annually or a sizeable percent of the foundation's annual giving, and (3) grants were for religious purposes specifically and not for religious-sponsored organizations such as schools and welfare groups. Using new information gathered from COMSEARCH printouts and the 10th edition of the *Foundation Directory* as verified by a review of IRS returns, 16 new entries were made to the present edition, while 7 previously listed entries were dropped because the foundations did not meet the above criteria.

The result is this list, which includes the largest foundations in the nation with an interest in religion, as well as some smaller foundations with almost exclusive interest in religion. The foundations fall into three broad categories (and some overlap into more than one of these divisions):

(1) Foundations almost solely devoted to religious funding.

(2) Large foundations with a sizeable amount of funding in the religious area, although religion is only one area of interest.

(3) Foundations which fund religious activities only in their locale or as a secondary area of funding interest.

This list does not include many foundations which give grant money to religious organizations for education, health, social welfare, or other "secular" programs. Those religious institutions seeking grant support for such programs are advised to consult the subject index of the latest edition of the *Foundation Directory*, the subject index of the *Foundation Center Source Book Profiles*, the appropriate COMSEARCH printout, and other reference sources found at the Foundation Center libraries and cooperating libraries identified in this guide.

The list also may not include the names of many small foundations which support religious activities in their own locale. These may be found in the various state directories.

Warning! Take this list for what it is—a compilation of the foundations with a past history of funding religious organizations. It should be a timesaver as it gives the grant seeker a starting place when searching for religious grants from among the 23,600 foundations. However, remember to do further research on the foundations that might fund your project. You cannot be sure until you do your homework.

Protestant Foundations

Alabama

CHRISTIAN WORKERS FOUNDATION, THE
3577 Bankhead Avenue
Montgomery, AL 36111
Contact Person: Allen W. Mathis, Jr., Director
Geographic Giving Pattern: National
Special Interest: Evangelical organizations
Assets: $2,556,796
Grant Range: $94,733 - $1,000
Limitation: No grants to individuals

MITCHELL FOUNDATION, INC., THE
2405 First National Bank Building
P.O. Box 1126
Mobile, AL 36601
(205) 432-1711
Contact Person: M.L. Screven, Jr., Director
Geographic Giving Pattern: Primarily local
Special Interest: Religious welfare agencies, Protestant church support
Assets: $7,592,825
Grant Range: $85,000 - $100

Arizona

GOPPERT FOUNDATION, THE
8336 Calle de Alegria
Scottsdale, AZ 85255
(602) 858-7043
Contact Person: Thomas A. Goppert, Goppert Foundation, P.O. Box 8743, Kansas City, MO 64114

Geographic Giving Pattern: Eastern Kansas, Western Missouri and Maricopa County, Arizona
Special Interest: Higher education, hospitals, church support
Assets: $3,351,508
Grant Range: $60,000 - $1,000
Limitation: No grants to individuals

TELL FOUNDATION, THE
20 Biltmore Estates
Phoenix, AZ 85016

Contact Person: Andrew P. Tell, President
Geographic Giving Pattern: Primarily local
Special Interest: To support Protestant churches and church-related institutions
Assets: $2,016,335
Grant Range: $60,000 - $25

Arkansas

JONES (THE HARVEY AND BERNICE) FOUNDATION
P.O. Box 233
Springdale, AR 72764
(501) 751-2730

Contact Person: Harvey Jones, Chairman
Geographic Giving Pattern: Primarily local
Special Interest: Protestant churches and church organizations
Assets: $4,304,942
Grant Range: $150,000 - $12

MURPHY FOUNDATION, THE
Murphy Building
El Dorado, AR 71730
(501) 862-6411

Contact Person: Lucy A. Ring, Secretary
Geographic Giving Pattern: Primarily local
Special Interest: Higher education - scholarships, Protestant church support and youth agencies
Assets: $9,778,237
Grant Range: $120,000 - $50

STURGIS (THE ROY AND CHRISTINE) CHARITABLE AND EDUCATIONAL TRUST
P.O. Box 92
Malvern, AR 72104
(501) 332-3506

Contact Person: Katie Speer, Trustee
Geographic Giving Pattern: Primarily local
Special Interest: Protestant church support, hospitals, youth and social agencies, education
Assets: $11,135,200
Grant Range: $58,000 (Denominational Giving)

California

AHMANSON FOUNDATION, THE
3731 Wilshire Boulevard
Los Angeles, CA 90010
(213) 383-1381

Contact Person: Kathleen A. Gilcrest, Vice-President and Secretary
Geographic Giving Pattern: Largely local
Special Interest: Broad - emphasis on education, arts and humanities, medicine and health and religious organizations
Assets: $211,855,588
Grant Range: $650,000 - $500; average $5,000 - $15,000
Limitation: No grants to individuals

ARTEVEL FOUNDATION
c/o Security Pacific Plaza
333 S. Hope St., Suite 3710
Los Angeles, CA 90071

Contact Person: George R. Phillips, Secretary-Treasurer
Geographic Giving Pattern: National, international
Special Interest: Protestant evangelical and missionary programs
Assets: $1,776,839
Limitation: Does not accept unsolicited applications for funds

ATKINSON FOUNDATION
10 W. Orange Avenue S.
S. San Francisco, CA 94080
(415) 876-1559

Contact Person: Donald K. Grant, Treasurer
Geographic Giving Pattern: Northern California and overseas
Special Interest: Methodist church, divisions of World Missions also activities of Willamette Unversity
Assets: $15,406,338
Grant Range: $12,000 - $1,000 (Religious)

ATKINSON (MYRTLE L.) FOUNDATION
c/o Mrs. Elizabeth A. Whitsett
P.O. Box 688
La Canada, CA 91011
(213) 790-7029

Contact Person: Mrs. Elizabeth A. Whitsett, President
Geographic Giving Pattern: National, international
Special Interest: Evangelical church unity. Also to "encourage and promote religious, scientific, technical and all other kinds of education, enlightenment and research"
Assets: $19,688,079
Grant Range: $15,000 - $1,000 (Religious)

BERRY (THE LOWELL) FOUNDATION
One Kaiser Plaza, Suite 890
Oakland, CA 94612
(415) 452-0433

Contact Person: John C. Branagh, President
Geographic Giving Pattern: Alameda/Contra Costa area
Special Interest: Evangelical Protestant church-related programs and institutions
Assets: $13,792,310
Grant Range: $136,000 - $60

BULL (THE HENRY W.) FOUNDATION
c/o Wells Fargo Bank
420 Montgomery No. 954
San Francisco, CA 94163
(415) 396-3105

Contact Person: James W.Z. Taylor, Administrator
Geographic Giving Pattern: Primarily local
Special Interest: Higher education, handicapped, church support
Assets: $3,753,590
Grant Range: $20,000 - $1,000

CADDOCK FOUNDATION, INC.
640 Sandalwood Court
Riverside, CA 92507
(714) 684-6326

Contact Person: Richard E. Caddock, President
Geographic Giving Pattern: Primarily local
Special Interest: Protestant religious associations, Bible studies
Assets: $1,262,773
Grant Range: $34,000 - $1,000

COBURN (THE MAURINE CHURCH) CHARITABLE TRUST
c/o Wells Fargo Bank, Trust Department
P.O. Box 2229
Monterey, CA 93940

Contact Person: Milton C. Coburn, Trustee
Geographic Giving Pattern: Primarily local
Special Interest: Protestant church-related institutions

Assets: $5,022,958
Limitation: Funds are presently committed

CRUMMEY (VIVIAN G.) BENEVOLENT TRUST
1441 University Avenue
San Jose, CA 95126
(408) 296-6585

Contact Person: Carolyn H. Crummey, Trustee
Geographic Giving Pattern: Primarily local
Special Interest: United Methodist churches, theological education,
missionary programs

Assets: $788,104
Grant Range: $41,250 - $1,000

FOREST LAWN FOUNDATION
1712 So. Glendale Avenue
Glendale, CA 91205
(213) 254-3131

Contact Person: John Llewellyn, Vice-President
Geographic Giving Pattern: Primarily local
Special Interest: Religious institutions, higher education, health and
    welfare, hospitals

Assets: $3,557,759
Grant Range: $15,000 - $250

GILMORE (EARL B.) FOUNDATION
6301 W. Third Street
Los Angeles, CA 90048
(213) 939-1191

Contact Person: M.B. Hartman, Treasurer
Geographic Giving Pattern: Primarily local
Special Interest: Protestant church support, higher and secondary
education, health and youth agencies, hospitals

Assets: $2,361,368
Grant Range: $15,000 - $100
Limitation: No unsolicited applications accepted

GOSPEL FOUNDATION OF CALIFORNIA
1462 North Stanley Avenue
Hollywood, CA 90046
(213) 876-2172

Contact Person: Mary E. Liddecoat, President
Geographic Giving Pattern: Primarily in California
Special Interest: Christian religious, charitable, educational, evangelistic
and mission enterprises
Assets: $2,542,955
Grant Range: $25,000 - $115
Limitation: Funds indefinitely committed; no grant applications accepted

GREENVILLE FOUNDATION, THE
P.O. Box 885
Pacific Palisades, CA 90272
(602) 946-6644

Contact Person: Wm. Miles, Jr., Chairman
Special Interest: Protestant religious programs and higher education
including a school of theology
Assets: $1,608,857
Grant Range: $38,500 - $100

HELMS FOUNDATION, INC.
P.O. Box 312
Redwood Valley, CA 95470
(707) 485-7997

Contact Person: W.D. Manuel, Assistant Secretary
Geographic Giving Pattern: Primarily local
Special Interest: Protestant church support and religious education
Assets: $3,551,400
Grant Range: $7,000 - $350

JAMESON (J.W. AND IDA M.) FOUNDATION
P.O. Box 397
Sierra Madre, CA 91024
(213) 355-9673

Contact Person: Arthur W. Kirk, President
Geographic Giving Pattern: Primarily in California
Special Interest: Higher education including theological seminaries.
Also for Protestant church support
Assets: $660,065
Grant Range: $40,000 - $1,000

LLOYD (THE RALPH B.) FOUNDATION
9441 Olympic Boulevard
Beverly Hills, CA 90212
(213) 879-3080

Contact Person: Eleanor Dees, President
Geographic Giving Pattern: Primarily in California and Oregon
Special Interest: Protestant church support, education

Assets: $6,807,017
Grant Range: $100,000 - $50

MUNGER (ALFRED C.) FOUNDATION
c/o Richard D. Esbenshade
612 So. Flower Street, 5th floor
Los Angeles, CA 90017
(213) 624-7715

Contact Person: Charles T. Munger
Geographic Giving Pattern: Primarily local
Special Interest: Protestant religious organizations

Assets: $6,796,047
Grant Range: $60,500 - $100

MURDY FOUNDATION
1450 N. Tustin Ave., Suite 200
Santa Ana, CA 92701

Contact Person: John A. Murdy, Jr.
Geographic Giving Pattern: Primarily local
Special Interest: Higher education, Protestant church support, cultural programs

Assets: $2,182,547
Grant Range: $99,000 - $100

ORLETON TRUST FUND
1777 Borel Place, Suite 306
San Mateo, CA 94402
(415) 345-2818

Contact Person: Mrs. Jean Sawyer Weaver
Geographic Giving Pattern: Dayton, OH and San Mateo County, CA
Special Interest: Protestant church support, religious associations, education, welfare funds

Assets: $6,470,974
Grant Range: $13,010 - $1,000 (Religious Purposes)

SCHMIDT (MARJORIE MOSHER) FOUNDATION
2111 Palomar Airport Rd., Suite 370
Carlsbad, CA 92008
(619) 438-4300
Contact Person: Mark F. Scudder, Secretary
Geographic Giving Pattern: Nationwide
Special Interest: Christian religious organizations. Also social, health, welfare organizations and education
Assets: $2,069,275
Grant Range: $5,000 - $500

SMITH (THE MAY AND STANLEY) TRUST
c/o John P. Collins, Sr.
49 Geary Street, Suite 244
San Francisco, CA 94102
(415) 391-0292
Contact Person: John P. Collins, Sr.
Geographic Giving Pattern: San Francisco area. Also in England, Scotland, Canada and Australia
Special Interest: Church support and religious welfare funds
Assets: $1,964,075
Grant Range: $5,000 - $1,000
Limitation: Applicant must be a public charity, care and housing of disabled children, the blind or the aged

STAMPS (JAMES L.) FOUNDATION, INC.
P.O. Box 250
Downey, CA 90241
(213) 861-3112
Contact Person: Milan Green, Secretary
Geographic Giving Pattern: West Coast states and Arizona
Special Interest: Evangelical Protestant churches, seminaries, associations and programs
Assets: $10,033,112
Grant Range: $25,000 - $400

VOSE (CLARA EDITH) FOUNDATION
c/o Rimel and Rimel
1055 N. Main Street, Station 406
Santa Ana, CA 92701
(714) 547-7395
Contact Person: Jack J. Rimel, Secretary
Geographic Giving Pattern: Primarily local
Special Interest: Evangelical church support, youth agencies, missions

Assets: $983,913
Grant Range: $12,000 - $100

Connecticut

BISSELL (J. WALTON) FOUNDATION
One Constitution Plaza, 12th floor
Hartford, CT 06103
(203) 521-6528
Contact Person: Wm. C. Fenneman, Secretary, 29 Ten Acre Lane,
W. Hartford, CT
Geographic Giving Pattern: National
Special Interest: Protestant church support. Also higher education,
hospital, agencies for youth and the aged
Assets: $7,885,464
Grant Range: $29,512 - $500

FAIRCHILD (SHERMAN) FOUNDATION, THE
71 Arch Street
Greenwich, CT 06830
(203) 661-9360
Contact Person: Walter Burke, President
Geographic Giving Pattern: No stated limits
Special Interest: Theological education. Also social services
Assets: $164,450,449
Grant Range: $250,000 - $100,000

WHEELER (WILMOT) FOUNDATION, INC.
P.O. Box 429
Southport, CT 06490
(203) 295-1615
Contact Person: Wilmot F. Wheeler, Jr., President
Geographic Giving Pattern: Primarily local
Special Interest: Education, Protestant church support, hospital and
community funds
Assets: $1,421,332
Grant Range: $10,500 - $100

Delaware

KENT (THE ADA HOWE) FOUNDATION
100 West Tenth Street
Wilmington, DE 19801

Contact Person: John E. Connelly, President; 299 Park Avenue, 17th floor, New York, NY 10017
Geographic Giving Pattern: National
Special Interest: Religious organizations carrying on studies and practical work in comparative religions, church support
Assets: $5,026,175
Grant Range: $78,000 - $1,500

KENT-LUCAS FOUNDATION, INC.
101 Springer Building
3411 Silverside Road
Wilmington, DE 19801
(302) 478-4383
Contact Person: Mrs. Ezabeth K. Van Alen, President; (302) 478-6160
Geographic Giving Pattern: Primarily in Philadelphia, PA and in Maine and Florida
Special Interest: Protestant church support, hospitals, medical and health organizations
Assets: $1,972,111
Grant Range: $5,500 - $50
Limitation: No grants to individuals

LOVETT FOUNDATION, INC., THE
82 Governor Printz Blvd.
Claymont, DE 19703
(302) 798-6604
Contact Person: Marie J. Wermuth, Treasurer
Geographic Giving Pattern: Delaware and Pennsylvania
Special Interest: Protestant church support, education, cultural and civic affairs
Assets: $1,990,086
Grant Range: $7,500 - $50

District of Columbia

APPLEBY FOUNDATION, THE
c/o Trust Division, National Savings & Trust Bank
15th Street and New York Ave., N.W.
Washington, D.C. 20005
(202) 383-8538
Contact Person: Trust Div., National Savings & Trust Bank;
c/o Pat Praeger
Geographic Giving Pattern: Washington, D.C., Florida, Georgia

Special Interest: Protestant church support. Also higher education, hospitals, cultural programs
Assets: $4,668,539
Grant Range: $20,000 - $1,500

Florida

AURORA FOUNDATION, THE
P.O. Box 1848
Bradenton, FL 33506
(813) 748-4100
Contact Person: Anthony T. Rossi, Chairman
Geographic Giving Pattern: National
Special Interest: Missions and church support, primarily Protestant
Assets: $59,789,102
Grant Range: $100,000 - $5,000

BAKER (THE GEORGE T.) FOUNDATION, INC.
P.O. Box 6585
Surfside, FL 33154
Contact Person: Elizabeth J. Wright, Secretary-Treasurer
Geographic Giving Pattern: Dade County, FL; Blowing Rock, NC
Special Interest: Education, hospitals, health agencies and medical research, youth agencies, Protestant church support
Assets: $1,295,257
Grant Range: $18,100 - $100

BASTIEN (JOHN E. AND NELLIE J.) MEMORIAL FOUNDATION
6991 West Broward Blvd.
Ft. Lauderdale, FL 33317
(305) 791-0810
Contact Person: Foundation at above address
Geographic Giving Pattern: General, National
Special Interest: Church support - Lutheran and Catholic. Also higher education, health agencies, general welfare
Assets: $8,503,720
Grant Range: $25,000 - $50

BIBLE ALLIANCE
P.O. Box 1894
Bradenton, FL 33506
(813) 748-4100

Contact Person: Anthony T. Rossi, Chairman; 1115 - 6th Ave., Bradenton FL 33506
Special Interest: Production and distribution of recorded portions of the Bible and religious messages on cassette tapes in various languages for use in missionary outreach
Assets: $3,404,634
Grant Range: $200,674 - $25
Limitation: No unsolicited applications accepted

CRANE (RAYMOND E. AND ELLEN F.) FOUNDATION, THE
P.O. Box 25427
Tamarac, FL 33320
Contact Person: Foundation at above address
Geographic Giving Pattern: National, primarily in S.E. states
Special Interest: Higher education and community funds. Also cultural programs, health and Protestant church support
Assets: $2,153,779
Grant Range: $10,000 - $250
Limitation: No unsolicited applications accepted

DAVIS (ARTHUR VINING) FOUNDATIONS, THE
Haskell Building, Suite 520
Oak & Fisk Streets
Jacksonville, FL 32204
(904) 359-0670
Contact Person: Max Morris, Executive Director
Geographic Giving Pattern: National
Special Interest: Private higher education, medicine, religious and public television
Assets: $69,902,000
Grant Range: $247,000 - $2,000

DUDA FOUNDATION, THE
P.O. Box 257
Oviedo, FL 32765
Contact Person: Andrew Duda, Jr., President
Geographic Giving Pattern: National
Special Interest: Protestant church support and church-related organizations
Assets: $871,597
Grant Range: $116,000 - $1,000

FORD (JEFFERSON LEE), III MEMORIAL FOUNDATION, INC.
Sun Bank of Bal Harbour
Bal Harbour, FL 33154
(305) 865-9911
1101 17th Street, N.W.
Washington, D.C. 20036
Contact Person: Herbert L. Kurras, Senior Vice-President and Trust
Officer; Sun Bank/ Miami, 9600 Collins Ave., P.O. Box 546457, Bal
Harbour, FL 33154
Special Interest: Religious institutions, Christian and Jewish
Assets: $2,106,121
Grant Range: $10,000 - $500

Georgia

BRADLEY - TURNER FOUNDATION
P.O. Box 140
Columbia, GA 31902
(404) 322-7348
Contact Person: W. Bradley Turner, Chairman
Geographic Giving Pattern: Primarily local
Special Interest: Higher education, Protestant church support, youth and
social agencies
Assets: $19,474,333
Grant Range: $15,500 - $100 (Religious Giving)
Limitation: No grants to individuals

CALLAWAY (FULLER E.) FOUNDATION
209 Broome Street
P.O. Box 790
La Grange, GA 30240
(404) 884-7348
Contact Person: J.T. Gresham, Gen. Manager
Geographic Giving Pattern: Local
Special Interest: Religious and educational institutions
Assets: $22,141,738
Grant Range: $10,000 - $1,000
Limitation: No grants for endowment funds or research

CAMPBELL (J. BULOW) FOUNDATION
1401 Trust Company Tower
25 Park Place N.E.
Atlanta, GA 30303
(404) 658-9066

Contact Person: Morris S. Hale, Jr. Executive Director
Geographic Giving Pattern: Limited to Georgia, Alabama, Florida, North
Carolina, South Carolina and Tennessee
Special Interest: Southern Presbyterian Church - U.S.
Assets: $66,001,359
Grant Range: $250,000 - $25,000

DAY (CECIL B.) FOUNDATION, INC.
6025 The Corners Pkwy., Suite 201
Norcross, GA 30092
(404) 446-1500

Contact Person: Edward L. White, President
Geographic Giving Pattern: Primarily in N.E. states; special consideration
for GA
Special Interest: Protestant religious organizations, missionary programs,
church support
Assets: $15,107,084
Grant Range: $135,000 - $75
Limitation: No grants to individuals or endowment funds

GHOLSTON (J.K.) TRUST
P.O. Box 992
Athens, GA 30613
(404) 549-8700

Contact Person: Janey Cooley, Trust Officer - Citizen & Southern National
Bank, Athens, GA
Geographic Giving Pattern: Local, limited to Comer, GA area
Special Interest: Church support, primarily Baptist
Assets: $2,912,093
Grant Range: $3,000 - $100 (Religious)

ILLGES (A. & M.L.) MEMORIAL FOUNDATION, INC.
1345 Second Avenue
P.O. Box 103
Columbus, GA 31902

Contact Person: A. Illges; 1224 Peacock Ave., Columbus, GA;
(404) 323-5342
Geographic Giving Pattern: Local, Georgia
Special Interest: Church support
Assets: $2,444,454
Grant Range: $10,000 - $1,000

PATTERSON - BARCLAY MEMORIAL FOUNDATION, INC.
1020 Spring Street, N.W.
Atlanta, GA 30309
(404) 876-1022
Contact Person: Mrs. Lee Barclay Patterson Allen
Special Interest: Churches and allied organizations, schools, including
seminaries and schools of theology, primarily Protestant, some Roman
Catholic and Greek Orthodox
Assets: $4,095,195
Grant Range: $5,000- $1,000 (Religious)

PATTILLO FOUNDATION, THE
2053 Mountain Industrial Blvd.
Tucker, GA 30084
(404) 378-8844
Contact Person: H.G. Pattillo
Geographic Giving Pattern: Primarily local
Special Interest: Higher education and Protestant church support
Assets: $900,438
Grant Range: $570,007 - $100

PITTS (WILLIAM I.H. AND LULA E.) FOUNDATION
P.O. Box 4655
Atlanta, GA 30302
(404) 588-8544
Contact Person: Marvin R. Benson, Secretary
Geographic Giving Pattern: Georgia
Special Interest: Primarily Methodist church-related institutions
Assets: $7,140,563
Grant Range: $40,000 - $425 (Religious)
Limitation: No grants to individuals or for endowment funds

RAGAN & KING CHARITABLE FOUNDATION
P.O. Box 4148
Atlanta, GA 30302
Contact Person: First National Bank of Atlanta; Attn: Frank Rozelle
Geographic Giving Pattern: Primarily local
Special Interest: Baptist church support, religious organizations,
theological seminaries, higher education
Assets: $1,595,496
Grant Range: $30,000 - $12,000

RAINBOW FUND
P.O. Box 937
Fort Valley, GA 31030
(912) 825-2021

Contact Person: Albert L. Luce, Jr., Treasurer
Geographic Giving Pattern: National
Special Interest: Protestant church support, religious organizations, missionary programs, theological education

SEWELL (WARREN P. AND AVA F.) FOUNDATION
Bremen, GA 30110
(404) 537-2391

Contact Person: Raymond C. Otwell, Trustee
Geographic Giving Pattern: Local
Special Interest: Protestant churches, schools
Assets: $4,229,961
Grant Range: $85,000 - $500

WILSON (FRANCES WOOD) FOUNDATION, INC., THE
P.O. Box 33188
Decatur, GA 30033
(404) 634-3363

Contact Person: Emory K. Crenshaw, President
Geographic Giving Pattern: Primarily local
Special Interest: Christian Science church. Also Methodist church in Tennessee
Assets: $12,840,832
Grant Range: $100,000 - $544

Hawaii

ATHERTON FAMILY FOUNDATION
c/o Hawaiian Trust Company Limited
111 S. King Street
Honolulu, HI 96813
(808) 525-6512

Contact Person: Jane R. Smith, Secretary
Geographic Giving Pattern: Hawaii
Special Interest: Protestant church support, scholarships for Protestant ministers' children or for theological education
Assets: $29,174,042
Grant Range: $5,000 - $1,000 (Religious)

WILCOX (G.N.) TRUST
c/o Bishop Trust Company, Limited
P.O. Box 2390
Honolulu, HI 96804
(808) 523-2111
Contact Person: Mrs. Lois C. Loomis, Charitable Foundation office
Geographic Giving Pattern: Particularly Island of Kauai
Special Interest: Education and child welfare, Protestant church support
Assets: $9,235,993
Grant Range: $25,000 - $1,000 (Religious)

Illinois

BAUER (M.R.) FOUNDATION
209 S. La Salle Street, Room 777
Chicago, IL 60604
(312) 372-1947
Contact Person: Kent Lawrence, Treasurer
Geographic Giving Pattern: National
Special Interest: Higher education, Protestant church support
Assets: $29,146,709
Grant Range: $100,000 - $2,500

CROWELL (HENRY P. AND SUSAN C.) TRUST
Lock Box 442
Chicago, IL 60690
(312) 372-5202
Contact Person: Lowell L. Kline, Executive Secretary
Geographic Giving Pattern: National, international
Special Interest: To aid evangelical Christianity
Assets: $25,223,218
Grant Range: $25,000 - $5,000

HALES CHARITABLE FUND, INC.
120 West Madison Street, Suite 14-E
Chicago, IL 60602
(312) 641-7016
Contact Person: Wm. M. Hales, President
Geographic Giving Pattern: National
Special Interest: Protestant church organizations and health agencies
Assets: $4,283,822
Grant Range: $150,000 - $200 (Religious)
Limitation: No unsolicited applications accepted

HARPER (PHILIP S.) FOUNDATION
930 N. York Road
Hinsdale, IL 60521
(312) 325-3400

Contact Person: Charles C. Lamar, Secretary-Treasurer
Geographic Giving Pattern: National
Special Interest: Protestant church support
Assets: $3,153,016
Grant Range: $6,000 - $500 (Religious)

LAYMAN TURST FOR EVANGELISM
c/o Robert H. Langerhans, Trustee
2047 Vermont Street
Quincy, IL 62301
(217) 222-2517

Contact Person: Robert H. Langerhans
Special Interest: Protestant evangelical associations for missionary work
Assets: $1,484,837
Grant Range: $30,000 - $14,000

MARQUETTE CHARITABLE ORGANIZATION
2141 S. Jefferson Street
Chicago, IL 60616
(312) 226-3232

Contact Person: Betty Basile, Secretary-Treasurer
Geographic Giving Pattern: National
Special Interest: Christian religious organizations, churches, education
Assets: $6,418,880
Grant Range: $74,500 - $50

RHOADES (OTTO L. AND HAZEL T.) FUND
c/o Leo J. Carlin
8000 Sears Tower
Chicago, IL 60606
(312) 876-8000

Contact Person: Leo J. Carlin
Geographic Giving Pattern: Chicago
Special Interest: Religious support - Presbyterian church, Christian communications organizations
Assets: $1,606,739
Grant Range: $20,000 - $5,000

TYNDAL HOUSE FOUNDATION
336 Gundersen Drive, Box 80
Wheaton, IL 60187
(312) 293-0179
Contact Person: Mary Kleine Yehling, Executive Director
Geographic Giving Pattern: National
Special Interest: Missions, evangelical organizations, Christian literature
projects and Bible translation
Assets: $268,975
Grant Range: $135,000 - $300
Limitation: Applications severely restricted; new grants awarded on a
limited basis; application form required

WERNER (CLARA AND SPENCER) FOUNDATION, INC.
616 S. Jefferson Street
Paris, IL 61944
Contact Person: Clara B. Werner, Chairman
Geographic Giving Pattern: National
Special Interest: Lutheran churches and programs including theological
education
Assets: $9,537,584
Grant Range: $50,000 - $5,000
Limitation: No grants to individuals

Indiana

BALL BROTHERS FOUNDATION
520 Merchants Bank Building
Muncie, IN 47305
(317) 747-0948
Contact Person: Douglas A. Bakken, Executive Director
Geographic Giving Pattern: Indiana
Special Interest: Educational, cultural, religious organizations
Assets: $57,049,000
Grant Range: $6,000 - $1,000 (Denominational)
Limitation: No grants to individuals

SMOCK (FRANK L. AND LAURA L.) FOUNDATION
c/o Lincoln National Bank & Trust Co.
116 E. Berry Street
Fort Wayne, IN 46802
(219) 423-6496

Contact Person: Lincoln National Bank & Trust Co.
Geographic Giving Pattern: Indiana
Special Interest: Presbyterian churches, a college, and ailing or needy elderly people
Assets: $5,325,192
Grant Range: $18,500 - $500

THRUSH (H.A.) FOUNDATION, INC.
P.O. Box 185
Peru, IN 46970
(317) 473-6765

Contact Person: Robert Thompson, Secretary
Geographic Giving Pattern: Primarily local
Special Interest: Protestant church support. Also higher education, health agencies, cultural programs
Assets: $2,543,646
Grant Range: $19,299 - $50

Iowa

E & M CHARITIES
c/o C. Maxwell Stanley
Stanley Building
Muscatine, IA 52761

Contact Person: C. Maxwell Stanley, President
Geographic Giving Pattern: National
Special Interest: Higher education, a Catholic mission, Protestant churches particularly Methodist
Assets: $751,212
Grant Range: $10,000 - $200
Limitation: No unsolicited applications accepted

Kansas

WIEDEMANN (K.T.) FOUNDATION, INC.
300 Page Court
Wichita, KS 67202
(316) 265-9311

Contact Person: Kenneth Pringle, Secretary
Geographic Giving Pattern: Primarily local
Special Interest: Church support
Assets: $18,817 (Market Value) plus $531,900 (Gifts Received)
Grant Range: $20,525 - $10 (Protestant Giving)
Limitation: No grants to individuals

Kentucky

COOKE (V.V.) FOUNDATION CORPORATION
3901 Atkinson Drive, Suite 409
Louisville, KY 40218
(502) 459-3968
Contact Person: Charles H. Wells, Executive Secretary
Geographic Giving Pattern: Primarily local
Special Interest: Baptist church support and higher education
Assets: $4,859,603
Grant Range: $33,415 - $100 (Religious)
Limitation: Contributions made only to pre-selected organizations. Unsolicited applications not accepted

HOUCHENS FOUNDATION, INC.
900 Church Street
Bowling Green, KY 42101
(502) 843-3252
Contact Person: Roger M. Page
Geographic Giving Pattern: Primarily local
Special Interest: Church support
Assets: $3,467,427
Grant Range: $21,350 - $10

LA VIERS (HARRY AND MAXIE) FOUNDATION, INC.
P.O. Box 332
Irvine, KY 40336
(606) 723-5111
Contact Person: Barbara P. La Viers, Secretary-Treasurer
Geographic Giving Pattern: Primarily local - Rural Eastern Kentucky
Special Interest: Protestant church support, higher education
Assets: $1,905,286
Grant Range: $20,000 - $500
Limitation: No grants to individuals

Louisiana

FRAZIER FOUNDATION, INC.
P.O. Box 1175
Minden, LA 71055
(318) 377-0182
Contact Person: James Walter Frazier, Jr., President
Geographic Giving Pattern: National

Special Interest: Church of Christ churches, missions, religious organizations, educational institutions
Assets: $5,397,462
Grant Range: $97,185 - $800
Limitation: No grants to individuals or for endowment funds

WHELESS FOUNDATION, THE
c/o Commercial National Bank in Shreveport
P.O. Box 21119
Shreveport, LA 71152
(318) 226-4631

Contact Person: Nicholas H. Wheless, Jr., Chairman
Geographic Giving Pattern: Primarily local
Special Interest: Church support
Assets: $2,906,210
Grant Range: $25,750 - $100

Maryland

CLARK-WINCHCOLE FOUNDATION
4550 Montgomery Ave., Suite 345N
Bethesda, MD 20814
(301) 654-3607

Contact Person: Laura E. Phillips, President
Geographic Giving Pattern: Primarily Washington, D.C. area
Special Interest: Higher education - all denominations, health and youth agencies, medical research and hospitals, Protestant church support
Assets: $22,304,884
Grant Range: $365,000 - $20,000

M.E. FOUNDATION, THE
Rutherford Plaza
7133 Rutherford Road
Baltimore, MD 21207

Contact Persons: Miss F. Carroll Brown, Vice-President and Treasurer; Mrs. Margaret Brown Trimble, President and Secretary
Geographic Giving Pattern: National, international
Special Interest: Protestant evangelistic missionary work and Bible studies
Assets: $10,813,214
Grant Range: $68,000 - $5,000

Michigan

CHAMBERLIN (GERALD W.) FOUNDATION INC.
500 Stephenson Highway, Suite 405
Troy, MI 48083
(313) 585-5290
Geographic Giving Pattern: Catherine M. Hoyer, Secretary
Geographic Giving Pattern: Primarily local
Special Interest: Protestant church support, youth agencies, higher and secondary education
Assets: $1,981,975
Grant Range: $10,000 - $200
Limitation: Contributions to pre-selected organizations only. No unsolicited applications accepted

COOK (PETER C. AND EMAJEAN) CHARITABLE TRUST
c/o Peter C. Cook
2660 28th Street, S.E.
Grand Rapids, MI 49506
(616) 949-7788
Contact Person: Peter C. Cook, Trustee
Geographic Giving Pattern: Primarily local
Special Interest: Protestant religious organizations, theological seminary, higher education
Assets: $1,547,536
Grant Range: $7,500 - $1,000

DE VOS (RICHARD AND HELEN) FOUNDATION, THE
7154 Windy Hill Road, S.E.
Grand Rapids, MI 49506
Contact Person: Richard M. De Vos, President
Geographic Giving Pattern: National
Special Interest: Evangelical organizations and churches
Assets: $12,900,052
Grant Range: $124,000 - $100 (Christian Giving)

GERSTACKER (ROLLIN M.) FOUNDATION, THE
P.O. Box 1945
Midland, MI 48640
Contact Person: E.N. Brandt, Secretary
Geographic Giving Pattern: Primarily in MI and OH
Assets: $25,190,987
Grant Range: $10,000 - $1,000 (Theological Education)

HERRICK FOUNDATION
2500 Comerica Building
Detroit, MI 48226
(313) 963-6420

Contact Person: Emmett E. Eagan, Vice-President and Secretary
Geographic Giving Pattern: Primarily local, some national
Special Interest: Protestant church support, health and welfare agencies, higher and secondary education
Assets: $134,305,920
Grant Range: $75,000 - $2,000 (Protestant Church Support)
Limitation: No grants to individuals

LA-Z-BOY CHAIR FOUNDATION
1284 N. Telegraph Road
P.O. Box 713
Monroe, MI 48161
(313) 242-1444

Contact Person: Herman Gertz, Administrator
Geographic Giving Pattern: National (in areas of company operations)
Special Interest: Church support
Assets: $5,885,419
Grant Range: $7,500 - $1,000 (Religious)

PAGEL (WILLIAM M. AND MARY E.) TRUST
c/o National Bank of Detroit
611 Woodward Avenue
Detroit, MI 48232
(313) 225-2764

Contact Person: Edwin R. Stroh, III, Manager, National Bank of Detroit
Geographic Giving Pattern: Local, Detroit
Special Interest: Protestant church support
Assets: $4,352,039
Grant Range: Two of $29,500 each (Religious)

Mississippi

COMMUNITY FOUNDATION, INC., THE
P.O. Box 924
Jackson, MS 39205

Contact Person: W.K. Paine, President-Treasurer
Geographic Giving Pattern: Primarily local
Special Interest: Protestant religious organizations, higher education and social agencies

Assets: $3,530,350
Grant Range: $20,000 - $500

Missouri

PILLSBURY FOUNDATION, THE
Six Oakleigh Lane
St. Louis, MO 63124

Contact Person: Joyce S. Pillsbury, President
Geographic Giving Pattern: Local, some national
Special Interest: Higher education, Baptist church support and religious organizations
Assets: $12,472,527
Grant Range: $72,200 - $100 (Religious)

WOLFF (JOHN M.) FOUNDATION, THE
c/o Tower Grove Bank and Trust Company
3134 South Grand Boulevard
St. Louis, MO 63118

Contact Person: Edith D. Wolff, Trustee
Geographic Giving Pattern: Primarily local
Special Interest: Church support, higher education, health agencies
Assets: $1,481,600
Grant Range: $25,000 - $250

New Jersey

KIRBY (F.M.) FOUNDATION, INC.
17 De Hart Street
Morristown, NJ 07960
(201) 538-4800

Contact Person: F.M. Kirby, II, President
Geographic Giving Pattern: Primarily New Jersey, New York, Pennsylvania
Special Interest: Education, church support, church-related organizations
Assets: $111,598,497
Grant Range: $22,000 - $350 (Denominational Giving)
Limitation: No grants to individuals

WILLITS FOUNDATION, THE
731 Central Avenue
Murray Hill, NJ 07974
(201) 277-8259

Contact Person: Mrs. Emily D. Lawrence
Geographic Giving Pattern: New Jersey, Georgia, Maine, New Mexico, New York and Massachusetts
Special Interest: Protestant church support, theological seminaries, higher education especially for the ministry
Assets: $2,477,433
Grant Range: $5,000 - $1,000 (Religious)

New York

BAIRD FOUNDATION, THE
1880 Elmwood Avenue
Buffalo, NY 14207
(716) 876-8100

Contact Person: William C. Baird, Manager
Geographic Giving Pattern: Primarily Erie County, New York
Special Interest: Episcopal church support
Assets: $5,650,599
Grant Range: $10,000 - $1,000
Limitation: No grants to individuals

CHATLOS FOUNDATION, INC., THE
2 Pennsylvania Plaza, Room 2121
New York, NY 10001
(212) 736-4343

Contact Person: William J. Chatlos, President
Geographic Giving Pattern: National
Special Interest: Higher education including religious education and religious associations
Assets: $51,331,730
Grant Range: $130,000 - $1,000
Limitation: No grants to individuals

DEWAR (JAMES AND JESSIE SMITH) FOUNDATION, INC.
c/o Ruston R. Henderson
45 Dietz Street
Oneonta, NY 13820

Contact Person: Ruston R. Henderson, President and Treasurer
Geographic Giving Pattern: Primarily local
Special Interest: Religious, charitable, cultural, educational purposes
Assets: $14,406,121
Grant Range: $6,000 - $1,000 (Religious)

KLEE (CONRAD AND VIRGINIA) FOUNDATION, INC., THE
c/o Clayton M. Axtell, Jr.
700 Security Mutual Building
Binghamton, NY 13901
(607) 772-2261
Contact Person: Clayton M. Axtell, Jr., President
Geographic Giving Pattern: Local, Broom County, Guilford in Chenango County
Special Interest: Community funds, Protestant church support, higher education
Assets: $3,733,407
Grant Range: $55,000 - $400
Limitation: No grants to individuals

KNOX FAMILY FOUNDATION
P.O. Box 387
Johnstown, NY 12095
Contact Person: John B. Knox, Chairman
Geographic Giving Pattern: National
Special Interest: Educational, civic, medical, Protestant church support
Assets: $3,260,031
Grant Range: $2,000 - $200 (Religious)

MOSTYN FOUNDATION, INC.
c/o James C. Edwards, Inc.
805 Third Avenue, 8th floor
New York, NY 10022
(212) 832-3919
Contact Person: Mrs. Whitney B. Atwood, President
Geographic Giving Pattern: National
Special Interest: Church support, evangelical organizations
Assets: $2,383,830
Grant Range: $40,000 - $1,000
Limitation: No grants to individuals

PALMER (FRANCIS ASBURY) FUND
c/o William A. Chisolm
47 E. 88th Street
New York, NY 10028
(212) 348-3100
Contact Person: William A. Chisolm, Secretary
Geographic Giving Pattern: National, international

Special Interest: Home missions and educational institutions, Christian ministers and workers, establishment of Bible teaching in colleges and schools, theological education
Assets: $1,910,240
Grant Range: $10,000 - $5,000
Limitation: No grants to individuals

SPRAGUE (SETH) EDUCATIONAL AND CHARITABLE FOUNDATION, THE
c/o U.S. Trust Company of New York
45 Wall Street
New York, NY 10005
(212) 425-4500

Contact Person: Mrs. Maureen Augusciak, Vice-President
Geographic Giving Pattern: New York and Massachusetts
Special Interest: Church support, theological seminaries, education, medical research, aid to the handicapped
Assets: $25,072,012
Grant Range: $5,000 - $1,000 (Denominational Giving)
Limitation: No grants to individuals

WALKER (GEORGE HERBERT) FOUNDATION, THE
c/o Convoy Hewitt O'Brien and Boardman
100 Park Avenue, 10th floor
New York, NY 10017
(212) 309-1000

Contact Person: Winslow M. Lovejoy
Geographic Giving Pattern: Eastern United States
Special Interest: Higher and secondary education, Protestant church support
Assets: $1,057,211
Grant Range: $17,000 - $500

WENDT (MARGARET L.) FOUNDATION, THE
1320 Liberty Bank Building
Buffalo, NY 14202
(716) 855-2146

Contact Person: Robert J. Kresse, Secretary
Geographic Giving Pattern: Primarily local
Special Interest: Lutheran church support. Also religious organizations
Assets: $24,626,091
Grant Range: $56,855 - $5,000 (Religious)
Limitation: No grants to individuals

North Carolina

ANDERSON (ROBERT C. AND SADIE G.) FOUNDATION
c/o North Carolina National Bank
Charlotte, NC 28255
(704) 374-5721

Contact Person: John F. Renger, Jr.
Geographic Giving Pattern: North Carolina
Special Interest: Presbyterian causes or institutions

Assets: $1,767,663
Grant Range: $55,000 - $1,500
Limitation: No grants to individuals

BELK FOUNDATION TRUST, THE
P.O. Box 31788
Charlotte, NC 28231

Contact Person: Thomas A. Belk, Chairman
Geographic Giving Pattern: North Carolina and South Carolina
Special Interest: Protestant church support, higher education

Assets: $12,969,750
Grant Range: $100,000 - $400

CANNON FOUNDATION, INC., THE
P.O. Box 548
Concord, NC 28026-0548

Contact Person: Dan L. Gray, Executive Director
Geographic Giving Pattern: Primarily local
Special Interest: Protestant church support, schools, hospitals

Assets: $68,002,884
Grant Range: $25,000 - $500 (Denominational Giving)

DOVER FOUNDATION, INC., THE
P.O. Box 208
Shelby, NC 28150

Contact Person: Charles I. Dover, President
Geographic Giving Pattern: Primarily local
Special Interest: Protestant church support. Also higher and secondary education

Assets: $6,968,810
Grant Range: $14,100 - $100 (Religious)

MORGAN TRUST FOR CHARITY, RELIGION AND EDUCATION
Laurel Hill, NC 28351
(919) 462-2016

Contact Person: James L. Morgan, Chairman
Geographic Giving Pattern: Primarily local
Special Interest: Higher education, a theological seminary, Protestant church support
Assets: $5,075,435
Grant Range: $12,500 - $100 (Religious)
Limitation: No grants to individuals

RICHARDSON (MARY LYNN) FUND, THE
P.O. Box 20124
Greensboro, NC 27420
(919) 274-5471

Contact Person: Bess R. Boney, Trustee
Geographic Giving Pattern: International
Special Interest: Foreign missions for religious, charitable or educational application
Assets: $2,042,286
Grant Range: $10,000 - $500

STOWE (ROBERT LEE), JR. FOUNDATION, INC.
P.O. Box 351
Mil Office Building
Belmont, NC 28012
(704) 825-5314

Contact Person: Robert Lee Stowe, Jr., President
Geographic Giving Pattern: Primarily local
Special Interest: Church support, child welfare, education
Assets: $2,071,907
Grant Range: $58,629 - $100

Ohio

AUSTIN MEMORIAL FOUNDATION, THE
3650 Mayfield Road
Cleveland Heights, OH 44118

Contact Person: Donald G. Austin, Jr., President
Geographic Giving Pattern: Primarily local
Special Interest: Higher and secondary education, hospitals, Protestant church support
Assets: $4,679,138
Grant Range: $50,000 - $500
Limitation: No grants to individuals

CROSSET CHARITABLE TRUST, THE
205 Central Avenue
Cincinnati, OH 45202
(513) 421-5511
Contact Person: Richard B. Crosset, Trustee
Geographic Giving Pattern: Primarily local
Special Interest: Religious, charitable, educational purposes
Assets: $3,245,952
Grant Range: $10,000 - $1,000

MLM CHARITABLE FOUNDATION
410 United Savings Building
Toledo, OH 43604
(419) 255-0500
Contact Person: Charles A. McKenny
Geographic Giving Pattern: National
Special Interest: Higher education, Protestant churches and ministries
Assets: $1,104,182
Grant Range: $24,000 - $1,000 (Religious)
Limitation: No grants to individuals

MOORES (HARRY C.) FOUNDATION, THE
c/o F.E. Caldwell
866 Clubview Boulevard
Worthington, OH 43085
(614) 846-0389
Contact Person: William H. Leighner, Secretary; 100 E. Broad St.,
Columbus, OH 43215
Geographic Giving Pattern: Primarily Columbus, Ohio, area
Special Interest: Rehabilitation of the handicapped, Protestant church support, hospitals, welfare organizations and cultural programs
Assets: $8,624,152
Grant Range: $15,000 - $1,000 (Protestant Churches)
Limitation: No grants to individuals or for endowment funds

TELL (PAUL P.) FOUNDATION
2762 Mayfair Road
Akron, OH 44312
(216) 614-7531
Contact Person: Paul P. Tell, Jr., President
Geographic Giving Pattern: National
Special Interest: Furtherance of evangelical Christianity

Assets: $2,477,990
Grant Range: $25,200 - $100
Limitation: No grants to individuals. Applications for grants not invited

Oklahoma

BROADHURST FOUNDATION
5350 E. 46th Street, Suite 116
P.O. Box 35858
Tulsa, OK 74135
(918) 663-9251

Contact Person: Ann Shannon Cassidy, Chairman
Geographic Giving Pattern: Mid-west
Special Interest: Scholarship funds for students training for the Christian ministry, support for educational and religious institutions
Assets: $4,030,452
Grant Range: $33,804 - $100
Limitation: No grants to individuals

MABEE (J.E. AND L.E.) FOUNDATION, INC., THE
420 Williams Center Tower I
One West Third Street
Tulsa, OK 74103
(918) 584-4286

Contact Person: Guy R. Mabee, Chairman
Geographic Giving Pattern: OK, TX, KS, AR, MO, NM
Assets: $341,450,443
Grant Range: $600,000 - $8,000

TULSA ROYALTIES COMPANY
3229-A S. Harvard Avenue
Tulsa, OK 74135
(918) 747-5638

Contact Person: William S. Bailey, Jr., President
Geographic Giving Pattern: Primarily local
Special Interest: Higher education, hospitals, social agencies, Protestant church support
Assets: $2,300,153
Grant Range: $10,000 - $100
Limitation: No grants to individuals

Pennsylvania

ADAMS FOUNDATION, INC.
202 W. Fourth Street
Bethlehem, PA 18016
(215) 867-5000; Ext. 241
Contact Person: Nancy A. Taylor, President
Geographic Giving Pattern: National
Special Interest: Higher and secondary education, hospitals, Protestant church support
Assets: $737,414
Grant Range: $30,000 - $500
Limitation: Written requests accompanied by financial statements

ASPLUNDH FOUNDATION
Blair Mill Road
Willow Grove, PA 19090
Contact Person: Lester Asplundh, President
Geographic Giving Pattern: Primarily local
Special Interest: Protestant church support
Assets: $2,225,750
Grant Range: $50,000 - $1,000

CRAIG (EARLE M.) AND MARGARET PETERS CRAIG TRUST
c/o Mellon Bank
One Mellon Bank Center
Pittsburgh, PA 15258
(412) 234-5248
Contact Person: Edward S. McKenna, Asst. Vice-President
Geographic Giving Pattern: National
Special Interest: Higher education, Protestant churches and religious organizations
Assets: $3,593,981
Grant Range: $20,000 - $1,000 (Denominational Giving)
Limitation: Applications are not accepted. The family directs distribution of funds

CRAWFORD (E.R.) ESTATE TRUST FUND A
P.O. Box 487
McKeesport , PA 15134
Contact Person: Francis E. Neish, Trustee
Geographic Giving Pattern: Primarily McKeesport and Duquesne, Pennsylvania
Special Interest: Protestant church support

Assets: $5,075,906
Grant Range: 50,000 - $100

HUSTON FOUNDATION, THE
c/o The Glenmede Trust Co.
229 S. 18th Street
Philadelphia, PA 19103
(215) 875-3200

Contact Person: John Van Gorder
Geographic Giving Pattern: National
Special Interest: Evangelical organizations

Assets: $1,741,591
Grant Range: $7,500 - $1,000
Limitation: No grants to individuals

HILLMAN (HENRY L.) FOUNDATION, THE
2000 Grant Building
Pittsburgh, PA 15219
(412) 566-1480

Contact Person: Ronald W. Wertz, Executive Director
Geographic Giving Pattern: Primarily Pittsburgh
Special Interest: Episcopal church support

Assets: $6,928,561
Grant Range: $25,000 - $250
Limitation: No grants to individuals

PETERS (CHARLES F.) FOUNDATION
c/o Equibank
2 Oliver Plaza
Pittsburgh, PA 15222
(412) 288-5638

Contact Person: J. Charles Peterson, Administrator
Geographic Giving Pattern: McKeesport area
Special Interest: Protestant church support

Assets: $1,938,198
Grant Range: $5,000 - $250
Limitation: No grants to individuals

PEW (J. HOWARD) FREEDOM TRUST
c/o The Glenmede Trust Co,.
229 S. 18th Street
Philadelphia, PA 19103
(215) 875-3200

Contact Person: Fred H. Billups, Jr., Vice-President
Geographic Giving Pattern: National
Special Interest: Christian religious organizations and theological
seminaries
Assets: $276,703,999
Grant Range: $810,000 - $6,000 (Religious)
Limitation: No grants to individuals or for endowment funds

SCHAUTZ (WALTER L.) FOUNDATION, THE
1150 E. Grove Street
Dunmore, PA 18512
(717) 344-1174

Contact Person: Madalene Schautz, President
Geographic Giving Pattern: Local
Special Interest: Theological seminaries, church support
Assets: $1,761,971
Grant Range: $6,000 - $200
Limitation: Grants made only to pre-selected organizations

STACKPOLE-HALL FOUNDATION
19 N. St. Marys Street
St. Marys, PA 15857
(814) 781-7167

Contact Person: William C. Conrad, Executive Secretary
Geographic Giving Pattern: Primarily Pennsylvania, some in
Massachusetts, North Carolina, Connecticut, New York, Washington, D.C.
Special Interest: Religion, especially Episcopal, education, charity
Assets: $14,544,147
Grant Range: $36,279 - $4,676 (Religious)
Limitation: First priority people of Elk County, PA

Rhode Island

CHAMPLIN FOUNDATIONS, THE
P.O. Box 637
Providence, RI 02901
(401) 421-3719

Contact Person: David A. King, Executive Director
Geographic Giving Pattern: Primarily local
Assets: $110,979,215
Grant Range: $75,000 - $6,800
Limitation: No grants to individuals. No loans

HAFFENREFFER FAMILY FUND
c/o Fleet National Bank
100 Westminster Street
Providence, RI 02903
(401) 278-6697

Contact Person: Mr. Stanley C. Bodell; c/o Fleet National Bank
Geographic Giving Pattern: Rhode Island and southeastern New England
Special Interest: Protestant church support
Assets: $3,231,515
Grant Range: $35,000 - $50

South Carolina

BELK-SIMPSON FOUNDATION
P.O. Box 1449
Greenville, SC 29602

Contact Person: Mrs. Willou Bichel, Director; P.O. Box 528, Greenville, SC 29602
Geographic Giving Pattern: Local
Special Interest: Protestant church support and higher education
Assets: $2,297,953
Grant Range: $13,100 - $100
Limitation: No grants to individuals

SIMPSON FOUNDATION, THE
c/o C & S National Bank of South Carolina
P.O. Box 1449
Greenville, SC 29602
(801) 271-4112

Contact Person: Mrs. Willou Bichel, Director
Geographic Giving Pattern: Primarily North and South Carolina
Special Interest: Protestant church support and religious organizations
Assets: $1,658,526
Grant Range: $15,000 - $100

STEVENS (JOHN T.) FOUNDATION
P.O. Box 158
Kershaw, SC 29067
(803) 475-3655

Contact Person: John S. Davidson, President
Geographic Giving Pattern: Primarily local
Special Interest: Protestant church support

Assets: $2,838,834
Grant Range: $22,500 - $250

Tennessee

BROWN (DORA MACLELLAN) CHARITABLE TRUST, THE
1101 Maclellan Building
Chattanooga, TN 37402
(615) 266-5257
Contact Person: W. Henry Trotter, President
Geographic Giving Pattern: Primarily local, and the south east
Special Interest: Education, Protestant religious associations and hospitals
Assets: $8,832,935
Grant Range: $60,000 - $570 (Christian Giving)
Limitation: No grants to individuals

CHURCH OF CHRIST FOUNDATION, INC.
224 Second Avenue N.
P.O. Box 1301
Nashville, TN 37202
(615) 244-0600
Contact Person: Paul S. Hargis, President
Geographic Giving Pattern: National
Special Interest: Church of Christ-related organizations including churches, schools and colleges
Assets: $13,177,053
Grant Range: $85,000 - $1,000
Limitation: Applications for grants currently not invited

HYDE (J.R.) FOUNDATION, INC.
1991 Corporate Avenue
Memphis, TN 38132
Contact Person: Ms. Margaret Hyde, President; 3030 Poplar Ave., Memphis, TN 38111
Geographic Giving Pattern: Mid-South area of United States
Special Interest: Missions, church support, education
Assets: $12,326,125
Grant Range: $100,000 - $200

MACLELLAN FOUNDATION, INC., THE
Provident Building
Chattanooga, TN 37402
(615) 755-1291

Contact Person: Hugh O. Maclellan, Jr., President
Geographic Giving Pattern: Primarily local
Special Interest: Evangelical church support, theological seminaries
Assets: $93,848,396
Grant Range: $472,820 - $4,200 (Protestant Giving and Theological Education)

Texas

AKIN FOUNDATION, THE
P.O. Box 19429
Houston, TX 77024
(713) 932-6210

Contact Person: James D. Yates, Secretary
Geographic Giving Pattern: Texas
Special Interest: Aid to various Churches of Christ
Assets: $172,386
Grant Range: $10,000 - $900

ALLBRITTON FOUNDATION
5615 Kirby Drive, Suite 310
Houston, TX 77005
(713) 522-4921

Contact Person: Virginia L. White, Secretary-Treasurer
Geographic Giving Pattern: Texas, New York, Washington, D.C.
Special Interest: Christian religious organizations and education
Assets: $1,479 (M) plus $400,000 Gifts
Expended on 40 Grants: $255,600

BELL TRUST
10726 Plano Road
Dallas, TX 75238
(214) 349-0060

Contact Person: H.L. Packer, Trustee
Geographic Giving Pattern: National, international
Special Interest: Churches of Christ
Assets: $1,853,458
Grant Range: $6,000 - $500
Limitation: Grants made only to Churches of Christ

BIVINS (MARY E.) FOUNDATION
414 Polk Street
P.O. Box 708
Amarillo, TX 79105

Contact Person: Mr. Lindy Ward; 6214 Elmhurst, Amarillo, TX 79106
Geographic Giving Pattern: Primarily local
Special Interest: Christian colleges, social agencies, health care
Assets: $37,719,152
Grant Range: $175,000 - $945
Limitation: Recipient should be resident of Texas whose field and institution are religious. Submission dealdlne: prior to November each year for the following year

BROWN (M.K.) FOUNDATION, INC.
c/o Bill Waters
P.O. Box 662
Pampa, TX 79066-0662
(806) 669-6851
Contact Person: Bill W. Waters, Chairman
Geographic Giving Pattern: Primarily local
Special Interest: Protestant church support
Assets: $1,823,654
Grant Range: $132,000 - $250

FAIR (R.W.) FOUNDATION, THE
P.O. Box 689
Tyler, TX 75710
(214) 592-3811
Contact Person: Wilton H. Fair, President
Geographic Giving Pattern: Primarily local
Special Interest: Protestant church support and church-related programs
Assets: $14,911,664
Grant Range: $181,500 - $200 (Protestant Religious Activities)
Limitation: No grants to individuals

FIKES (LELAND) FOUNDATION, INC.
3206 Republic National Bank Tower
Dallas, TX 75201
(214) 754-0144
Contact Person: Nancy Solana, Research & Grant Administration
Geographic Giving Pattern: Primarily local
Special Interest: Protestant church support, medical and social research, education
Assets: $47,994,503
Grant Range: $41,008 - $1,000 (Protestant Giving)
Limitation: No grants to individuals

FLEMING FOUNDATION, THE
1007 Interfirst Fort Worth Building
Fort Worth, TX 76102
(817) 335-3741

Contact Person: G. Malcolm Louden, Asst. Secretary-Treasurer
Geographic Giving Pattern: Primarily local
Special Interest: Protestant church support and church-related activities including radio and TV programs, music, higher education
Assets: $10,640,881
Grant Range: $338,705 - $100 (Protestant Giving)
Limitation: No grants to individuals

HEATH (ED AND MARY) FOUNDATION
P.O. Box 338
Tyler, TX 75710
(214) 597-7435

Contact Person: W.R. Smith, Chairman
Geographic Giving Pattern: Primarily local
Special Interest: Church support
Assets: $2,025,015
Grant Range: $20,000 - $15

LE TOURNEAU FOUNDATION, THE
P.O. Box 736
Rockwall, TX 75087
(214) 722-8325

Contact Person: R.S. Le Tourneau, President
Special Interest: Evangelical Christian activities in foreign missions, evangelism, and education
Assets: $7,720,796
Grant Range: $48,284 - $500

MEADOWS FOUNDATION, INC.
Wilson Historic Block
2922 Swiss Avenue
Dallas, TX 75204
(214) 826-9431

Contact Person: Dr. Sally R. Lancaster
Geographic Giving Pattern: Limited to Texas
Assets: $324,123,001
Grant Range: $200,000 - $8,000
Limitation: No grants to individuals. No loans

MCCRELESS (SOLLIE AND LILLA) FOUNDATION FOR CHRISTIAN
EVANGELISM, CHRISTIAN MISSIONS AND CHRISTIAN EDUCATION
P.O. Box 2341
San Antonio, TX 78298
Contact Person: Marjorie Gerfen, Secretary
Geographic Giving Pattern: National, some emphasis on San Antonio
Special Interest: Protestant churches, theological education and
evangelical organizations
Assets: $3,653,632
Grant Range: $35,000 - $600

MCMILLAN (BRUCE), JR., FOUNDATION
P.O. Box 9
Overton, TX 75684
(214) 834-3148
Contact Person: Ralph Ward, President
Geographic Giving Pattern: Local, east Texas
Special Interest: Church support
Assets: $10,733,979
Grant Range: $15,600 - $500 (Protestant Churches)

OLDHAM LITTLE CHURCH FOUNDATION
5177 Richmond Avenue, Suite 1068
Houston, TX 77056
(713) 621-4190
Contact Person: Harry A. Kinney, Executive Vice-President
Geographic Giving Pattern: National, international
Special Interest: To aid small Protestant churches and religious educa-
tional institutions
Assets: $12,923,346
Grant Range: $5,000 - $123
Limitation: No grants to individuals

TRULL FOUNDATION, THE
404 Fourth Street
P.O. Box 1050
Palacios, TX 77465
(512) 972-5241
Contact Person: Coleen Claybourn, Trustee
Geographic Giving Pattern: National
Special Interest: Religious, educational, medical, evangelical purposes
Assets: $9,215,075
Grant Range: $7,500 - $400 (Religious)
Limitation: No grants to individuals

Virginia

ENGLISH (W.C.) FOUNDATION
1522 Main Street
Altavista, VA 24517
(804) 324-7241

Contact Person: W.C. English, Manager
Geographic Giving Pattern: Primarily local
Special Interest: Religious, educational, civic purposes
Assets: $3,758,619
Grant Range: $50,000 - $500

OLSSON (ELIS) MEMORIAL FOUNDATION
c/o Carle E. Davis
1400 Ross Building
Richmond, VA 23219

Contact Person: Sture G. Olsson, Manager
Geographic Giving Pattern: Primarily local
Special Interest: Protestant church support, higher and secondary education
Assets: $8,026,250
Grant Range: 30,000 - $100

TITMUS FOUNDATION, INC., THE
Route 1, Box 358
Sutherland, VA 23885
(804) 265-5834

Contact Person: Edward B. Titmus, President
Geographic Giving Pattern: Primarily local
Special Interest: Baptist church support and religious organizations
Assets: $8,121,697
Grant Range: $42,000 - 200 (Religious)

TREAKLE (J. EDWIN) FOUNDATION, INC., THE
Box 1157
Gloucester, VA 23601
(804) 693-3101

Contact Person: John W. Cooke, Treasurer
Geographic Giving Pattern: Primarily local
Special Interest: Protestant church support
Assets: $2,725,444
Grant Range: $8,400 - $200

Washington

STEWARDSHIP FOUNDATION, THE
P.O. Box 1278
Tacoma, WA 98401
(206) 272-8336

Contact Person: C. David Weyerhaeuser, Trustee
Geographic Giving Pattern: National, international
Special Interest: Protestant theological education and Christian evangelical activities
Assets: $47,715,891
Grant Range: $171,000 - $500
Limitation: No grants to individuals

Wisconsin

KURTH RELIGIOUS TRUST
11514 N. Port Washington Road, 13-W, Suite 106
Milwaukee, WI 53092
(414) 384-3030

Contact Person: Katherine Kurth, Manager
Geographic Giving Pattern: Primarily local
Special Interest: Lutheran church support and religious associations. Also higher education
Assets: $4,048,620
Grant Range: $65,500 - $10

RODDIS (HAMILTON) FOUNDATION, INC.
c/o Augusta D. Roddis
1108 E. Fourth Street
Marshfield, WI 54449

Contact Person: Augusta D. Roddis, Secretary-Treasurer
Geographic Giving Pattern: National
Special Interest: Episcopal church support, church-related institutions, medical research
Assets: $2,652,540
Grant Range: $13,000 - $250 (Relgious)
Limitation: No grants to individuals. No unsolicited applications accepted

SIEBERT LUTHERAN FOUNDATION, INC.
2600 North Mayfair Road, Suite 390
Wauwatosa, WI 53226
(414) 257-2656

Contact Person: Jack S. Harris, President
Geographic Giving Pattern: Primarily Wisconsin, some national
Special Interest: Lutheran churches, hospitals, colleges and schools, youth agencies and other religious welfare agencies
Assets: $39,793,027
Grant Range: $40,000 - $900 (Church Support)
Limitation: No grants to individuals. No grants for expenditure outside the U.S.

YOUNG (IRVIN L.) FOUNDATION, INC.
Snow Valley Ranch
Palmyra, WI 53156
(414) 495-2485
Contact Person: Mrs. Fern D. Young, President
Geographic Giving Pattern: International
Special Interest: Protestant medical missionary programs in Africa
Assets: $9,744,436
Grant Range: $110,000 - $500

Catholic Foundations

California

BURNS (FRITZ B.) FOUNDATION
4001 West Alameda Avenue, Suite 203
Burbank, CA 91505
(213) 938-7221

Contact Person: Mr. Joseph E. Rawlinson, President
Geographic Giving Pattern: Primarily local
Special Interest: Roman Catholic religious associations, hospitals, church support
Assets: $27,926,490
Grant Range: $100, 000 - $100

CALLISON FOUNDATION, THE
c/o Feeney, Sparks and Rudy
Hearst Building, Suite 1100
San Francisco, CA 94103
(415) 362-2981

Contact Person: Mrs. Dorothy Sola, Secretary
Geographic Giving Pattern: Primarily local
Special Interest: Roman Catholic religious associations, higher education
Assets: $4,237,755
Grant Range: $20,000 - $5,000

DOHENY (CARRIE ESTELLE) FOUNDATION
1010 S. Flower Street, Suite 400
Los Angeles, CA 90015
(213) 748-5111

Contact Person: Very Rev. W.G. Ward, C.M., Chairman
Geographic Giving Pattern: Local, primarily southern California
Special Interest: Roman Catholic churches and church-related organizations, hospitals, ophthalmological research, child welfare, education, community funds
Assets: $55,344,512
Grant Range: $1,465,333 - $250; $10,000 - $500 (General Range)

DRUM FOUNDATION, THE
c/o Wells Fargo Bank
420 Montgomery #954
San Francisco, CA 94163
(415) 396-3105

Contact Person: Ann Russell Miller
Geographic Giving Pattern: Usually limited to the Archdiocese of San Francisco
Special Interest: Roman Catholic church-related educational and charitable organizations
Assets: $3,471,457
Grant Range: $50,000 - $1,000
Limitation: No grants to individuals

GALLO (JULIO R.) FOUNDATION, THE
P.O. Box 1130
Modesto, CA 95353
(209) 579-3373

Contact Person: R.J. Gallo
Geographic Giving Pattern: Primarily local
Special Interest: Roman Catholic church support, religious associations, education
Assets: $3,997,627
Grant Range: $30,500 - $500

GELLERT (CARL) FOUNDATION, THE
2222 Nineteenth Avenue
San Francisco, CA 94116
(415) 566-4420

Contact Person: Peter J. Brusati, Secretary
Geographic Giving Pattern: Primarily local
Special Interest: The aged and hospitals. Also Roman Catholic church support, higher and secondary education
Assets: $7,583,468
Grant Range: $100,000 - $1,000

GLEASON (JAMES) FOUNDATION
Hearst Building, Suite 1200
Third and Market Streets
San Francisco, CA 94103
(415) 421-6995

Contact Person: Walter M. Gleason, President
Geographic Giving Pattern: Primarily local
Special Interest: Roman Catholic welfare funds and church support
Assets: $1,220,288
Grant Range: $50,000 - $500

GLEASON (KATHERINE) FOUNDATION
c/o Walter Gleason
Hearst Building, Suite 1200
Third and Market Streets
San Francisco, CA 94103
(415) 421-6995
Contact Person: Walter M. Gleason, President
Geographic Giving Pattern: World wide
Special Interest: Roman Catholic religious, welfare, educational and missionary endeavors
Assets: $2,628,039
Grant Range: $10,000 - $100

HALE (CRESCENT PORTER) FOUNDATION
220 Bush Street, Suite 1069
San Francisco, CA 94104
Contact Person: Melvin M. Swig, President
Special Interest: Higher education, hospitals and Roman Catholic religious organizations
Assets: $14,502,035
Grant Range: $10,000 - $1,000
Limitation: No grants to individuals. Apply by letter

HARNEY FOUNDATION, THE
923 Folsom Street
San Francisco, CA 94107
(415) 495-5352
Contact Person: Mr. Floyd S. Roberts, c/o Foundation
Geographic Giving Pattern: Primarily local
Special Interest: Roman Catholic religious, charitable and educational organizations. Also grants for medical and research organizations
Assets: $468,436
Grant Range: $60,000 - $6,000

HAYDEN (WILLIAM R.) FOUNDATION
110 West Las Tunis Drive, Suite A
San Gabriel, CA 91776
(213) 285-9891
Contact Person: William R. Hayden, President
Geographic Giving Pattern: Primarily local, some national
Special Interest: Religious, educational, medical organizations
Assets: $1,806,847
Grant Range: $20,000 - $200
Limitation: Contributions made to pre-selected organizations

LEAVEY (THOMAS AND DOROTHY) FOUNDATION
4680 Wilshire Boulevard
Los Angeles, CA 90010
(213) 936-5875

Contact Person: Dorothy Leavey, Vice-Presidnet
Geographic Giving Pattern: Primarily local
Special Interest: Roman Catholic church groups, hospitals, medical research, higher and secondary education
Assets: $56,933,409
Grant Range: $2,006,000 - $1,000; $100,000 - $10,000 (General Range)

LEONARDT FOUNDATION
1801 Avenue of the Stars, Suite 811
Los Angeles, CA 90067
(213) 556-3932

Contact Person: Felix S. McGinnis, President
Geographic Giving Pattern: Primarily local
Special Interest: Roman Catholic church support
Assets: $2,337,171
Grant Range: $20,000 - $500
Limitation: No grants to individuals

MARINI FAMILY TRUST
c/o Trust Dept., 9250 VIF
P.O. Box 37000
San Francisco, CA 94137

Contact Person: Trust Officer, Bank of America, NT-SA, Trust Dept., San Francisco, CA
Geographic Giving Pattern: Primarily local
Special Interest: Roman Catholic church support, education, social services
Assets: $2,283,773
Grant Range: $25,000 - $500

MULLER (FRANK), SR. FOUNDATION
c/o Norby, Sutherland & Muller
7080 Hollywood Boulevard, 318
Hollywood, CA 90028
(213) 463-8176

Contact Person: Frank Muller
Geographic Giving Pattern: Primarily local
Special Interest: Roman Catholic church support, higher and secondary education, social agencies, hospitals, cultural programs
Assets: $5,146,800
Grant Range: $25,000 - $25

MURPHY (DAN) FOUNDATION
P.O. Box 76026
Los Angeles, CA 90076
(213) 384-3036

Contact Person: Daniel J. Donohue
Geographic Giving Pattern: California, emphasis on Los Angeles
Special Interest: Roman Catholic educational, religious, charitable organizations
Assets: $99,533,713
Grant Range: $645,244 - $850 (Religious Giving)
Limitation: Because of ongoing commitments seldom able to consider unsolicited grant proposals

SHEA FOUNDATION, THE
655 Brea Canyon Road
Walnut, CA 91789
(714) 594-9500

Contact Person: John F. Shea, President
Geographic Giving Pattern: California
Special Interest: Roman Catholic church and religious associations. Also educational, civic, cultural endeavors and help for the Blind
Assets: $1,990,989
Grant Range: $15,000 - $600

VON DER AHE FOUNDATION
4605 Lankershim Boulevard, Suite 707
N. Hollywood, CA 91602
(213) 877-2454

Contact Person: Wilfred L. Von der Ahe   Wilfred L. von der Ahe
Geographic Giving Pattern: Primarily local, some national
Special Interest: Roman Catholic religious institutions and health and welfare services
Assets: $3,441,187
Grant Range: $30,000 - $500
Limitation: No grants to individuals. Giving primarily in CA

WELK (LAWRENCE) FOUNDATION
1299 Ocean Avenue, Suite 800
Santa Monica, CA 90401
(213) 451-5727

Contact Person: Shirley Fredricks, Executive Director
Geographic Giving Pattern: Primarily local
Special Interest: Education, cancer research, hospitals, Roman Catholic institutions, community funds

Assets: $888,125
Grant Range: $15,000 - $100

TRUST FUNDS, INC.
100 Broadway, Third Floor
San Francisco, CA 94111
(415) 434-3323

Contact Person: Albert J. Steiss
Geographic Giving Pattern: San Francisco Bay area
Special Interest: Roman Catholic institutions and projects which promote the religious, educational, and social welfare of all people
Assets: $3,039,745
Grant Range: $10,000 - $100

Colorado

MULLEN (JOHN K. AND CATHERINE S.) BENEVOLENT
CORPORATION, THE
1345 First National Bank Building
Denver, CO 80202
(303) 893-3151

Contact Person: Leon A. Lascor, Secretary
Geographic Giving Pattern: Primarily local
Special Interest: Public charities and educational institutions with emphasis on church-affiliated organizations
Assets: $3,241,039
Grant Range: $134,200 - $500
Limitation: No grants to individuals

WECKBAUGH (ELEANOR MULLEN) FOUNDATION
1779 South Monaco Parkway
Denver, CO 80224
(303) 756-0202

Contact Person: Patricia J. Lascor
Geographic Giving Pattern: Primarily local
Special Interest: Roman Catholic church support and welfare funds
Assets: $2,799,438
Grant Range: $30,000 - $1,500
Limitation: No grants to individuals

Connecticut

CASEY (ANNIE E.) FOUNDATION, THE
51 Weaver Street
Greenwich Office Park 5
Greenwich, CT 06830
(203) 622-6095
Contact Person: Frank A. Suchomel, Jr., Secretary
Geographic Giving Pattern: Connecticut and Seattle, Washington
Special Interest: Child welfare, specifically the care of foster children in Connecticut. Also Roman Catholic church support in Seattle, Washington
Assets: $142,629,923

DELL (HAZEL) FOUNDATION, THE
c/o Carroll, Lane & Reed
P.O. Box 771
Norwalk, CT 06852
(203) 853-6565
Contact Person: June M. Powers, President
Geographic Giving Pattern: National
Special Interest: Roman Catholic church support, hospitals, education, aid to the handicapped
Assets: $1,994,301
Grant Range: $19,700 - $100

HUISKING FOUNDATION, INC., THE
488 Main Avenue (Route 7)
P.O. Box 5100
Norwalk, CT 06856-5100
(203) 847-1191
Contact Person: William W. Huisking, Vice-President
Geographic Giving Pattern: General
Special Interest: Education, Roman Catholic church and welfare funds, hospitals and religious associations
Assets: $2,558,856
Grant Range: $3,500 - $250 (Religious Purposes)
Limitation: No grants to individuals

J.J.C. FOUNDATION, INC.
One Carney Road
West Hartford, CT 06110
(203) 246-6531

Contact Person: Miss Grace Carney
Geographic Giving Pattern: Primarily local
Special Interest: Emphasis on church support - all denominations. Also higher education, health agencies and community funds
Assets: $1,354,560
Grant Range: $5,000 - $100

SULLIVAN (RAY H. AND PAULINE) FOUNDATION
c/o Connecticut National Bank
777 Main Street
Hartford, CT 06115
(203) 728-2703

Contact Person: John C. Curtin
Geographic Giving Pattern: Diocese of Norwich, Connecticut
Special Interest: Roman Catholic charities and educational institutions
Assets: $5,816,114
Grant Range: $100,000 - $500
Limitation: Deadline for applications May 1

Delaware

LAFFEY-MCHUGH FOUNDATION
1220 Market Building
P.O. Box 2207
Wilmington, DE 19899
(302) 658-9141

Contact Person: Arthur G. Connolly, President
Geographic Giving Pattern: Primarily local
Special Interest: Roman Catholic church support and church-related institutions
Assets: $21,391,657
Grant Range: $30,000 - $5,000
Limitation: No grants to individuals

RASKOB FOUNDATION FOR CATHOLIC ACTIVITIES, INC.
P.O. Box 4019
Wilmington, DE 19807
(302) 655-4440

Contact Person: Gerard S. Garey, President
Geographic Giving Pattern: National, international
Special Interest: Institutions and organizations identified with the Roman Catholic church

Assets: $47,856,944
Grant Range: $10,000 - $500
Limitation: No grants to individuals

District of Columbia

DELMAR (CHARLES) FOUNDATION, THE
c/o John H. Doyle
918 Sixteenth Street, N.W., Suite 203
Washington, D.C. 20006
(202) 393-2266; (202) 293-2494
Contact Person: Elizabeth Adams DelMar
Geographic Giving Pattern: Washington, D.C., Puerto Rico, Latin America
Special Interest: Roman Catholic and Episcopalchurches, hospitals, welfare organizations
Assets: $1,922,000
Grant Range: $5,000 - $100

KENNEDY (JOSEPH P.), JR. FOUNDATION, THE
1350 New York Avenue, N.W., Suite 500
Washington, D.C. 20005
(202) 393-1250
Contact Person: Mrs. Eunice Kennedy Shriver, Executive Vice-President
Geographic Giving Pattern: No restrictions
Special Interest: Primarily concerned with the rights of the powerless, their treatment by social institutions, strengthening of the family, amelioration of conditions concerning individuals with mental retardation, and the ethical implications of genetic and biological discoveries
Assets: $18,054,555
Grant Range: $100,000 - $1,000

LOUGHRAN (MARY AND DANIEL) FOUNDATION, INC.
c/o American Security & Trust
15th Street & Pennsylvania Avenue, N.W.
Washington, D.C 20013
(202) 624-4283
Contact Person: Roberta Stearns, Asst. Administrator
Geographic Giving Pattern: Washington, D.C., Virginia, Maryland
Special Interest: Religious institutions, youth and social agencies, higher education
Assets: $11,094,044
Grant Range: $40,000 - $2,500

LOYOLA FOUNDATION, INC., THE
c/o Albert G. McCarthy III
305 C Street, N.E.
Washington, D.C. 20002
(202) 546-9400

Contact Person: Albert G. McCarthy III, Secretary
Geographic Giving Pattern: National, international, primarily in developing nations
Special Interest: Roman Catholic missionary work and other Catholic activities of interest to the trustees
Assets: $15,202,906
Grant Range: $40,000 - $250
Limitation: No grants to individuals

Florida

KOCH FOUNDATION, INC.
625-B N.W. 60th street
Gainesville, FL 32607
(904) 373-7491

Contact Person: Richard DeGraff
Geographic Giving Pattern: National
Special Interest: Roman Catholic religious organizations that propagate the faith
Assets: $43,007,762
Grant Range: $50,000 - $5,000
Limitation: No grants to individuals or endowment funds

LEWIS (FRANK J.) FOUNDATION
P.O. Box 9726
Riviera Beach, FL 33404

Contact Person: Edward D. Lewis, President
Geographic Giving Pattern: National
Special Interest: To foster, preserve and extend the Roman Catholic faith. Educational institutions, church support, religious orders, church-sponsored programs
Assets: $13,341,124
Grant Range: $100,000 - $200
Limitation: No grants to individuals or for endowment funds

Hawaii

HO (CHINN) FOUNDATION
239 Merchant Street
P.O. Box 2668
Honolulu, HI 96803
(808) 537-3891

Contact Person: Donald M. Wong, Treasurer
Geographic Giving Pattern: Hawaii
Special Interest: Higher education, Roman Catholic church support
Assets: $1,051,845
Grant Range: $10,000 - $250 (Religious)

Illinois

BOWYER (AMBROSE AND GLADYS) FOUNDATION, THE
135 S. La Salle Street, Suite 1500
Chicago, IL 60603
(312) 346-1030

Contact Person: D.T. Hutchison, President
Geographic Giving Pattern: National
Special Interest: Higher education, hospitals, welfare funds, Roman Catholic and Protestant religious organizations
Assets: $2,247,879
Grant Range: $5,000 - $1,000

CHRISTIANA FOUNDATION, INC.
69 W. Washington Street, Room 2700
Chicago, IL 60602
(312) 630-4400

Contact Person: Jerome A. Frazel, Jr., President
Geographic Giving Pattern: Primarily local
Special Interest: Roman Catholic community welfare organizations, secondary and higher education
Assets: $1,103,264
Grant Range: $2,000 - $500 (Religious)

CUNEO FOUNDATION, THE
9101 Greenwood Avenue, Suite 210
Niles, IL 60648
(312) 296-3351

Contact Person: John F. Cuneo, Jr., President
Geographic Giving Pattern: Primarily local

Special Interest: Roman Catholic religious associations, higher education and welfare funds
Grant Range: $18,000 - $100

FITZGERALD (FATHER JAMES M.) SCHOLARSHIP TRUST
c/o Commercial National Bank of Peoria
301 S. W. Adams Street
Peoria, IL 61613
(309) 655-5536

Contact Person: Rev. Francis Cahill
Geographic Giving Pattern: Illinois
Special Interest: Scholarships restricted to Illinois residents who are studying for the priesthood and attend a Catholic university or college
Assets: $1,048,814
Grant Range: $15,000 - $3,000

GALVIN (PAUL V.) TRUST
c/o Harris Trust & Savings Bank
111 W. Monroe Street
Chicago, IL 60603

Contact Person: Ellen A. Bechtold, 7E, Harris Trust & Savings Bank, P.O. Box 755, Chicago, IL 60690
Special Interest: Catholic religious organizations
Assets: $1,853,541
Grant Range: $200,000 - $1,000

GALVIN (ROBERT W.) FOUNDATION
1303 E. Algonquin Road
Schaumburg, IL 60196
(312) 576-5300

Contact Person: Robert W. Galvin, President
Geographic Giving Pattern: Primarily local
Special Interest: Higher education, aid to the handicapped, hospitals, church support and religious organizations
Assets: $5,207,885
Grant Range: $51,010 - $100
Limitation: No grants to individuals

JOYCE (JOHN M. AND MARY A.) FOUNDATION, THE
777 Joyce Road
Joliet, IL 60436
(815) 741-7733

Contact Person: William J. Davito, Secretary
Geographic Giving Pattern: National

Special Interest: Roman Catholic churches and religious societies
Assets: $3,458,477
Grant Range: $41,500 - $260

MAZZA FOUNDATION
c/o Cosmopolitan National Bank
801 N. Clark Street
Chicago, IL 60610
(312) 664-5200
Contact Person: Neil Vernasco, Asst. Secretary
Geographic Giving Pattern: Chicago
Special Interest: Churches, religious organizations, social agencies, Roman Catholic schools of theology
Assets: $6,930,336
Grant Range: $200,000 - $1,000 (Religious)

SCHMITT (ARTHUR J.) FOUNDATION
Two North La Salle Street, Suite 2010
Chicago, IL 60602
(312) 236-5089
Contact Person: John A. Donohue, Executive Secretary
Geographic Giving Pattern: Primarily local
Special Interest: Roman Catholic educational and religious institutions
Assets: $13,988,827
Grant Range: $10,000 - $2,500 (Denominational Giving)
Limitation: No grants to individuals

SIRAGUSA FOUNDATION, THE
840 N. Michigan Avenue, Suite 615
Chicago, IL 60611
(312) 280-0833
Contact Person: Melvin T. Tracht, Treasurer
Geographic Giving Pattern: Primarily Mid-west
Special Interest: Roman Catholic with some giving to Protestant churches, an Eastern Orthodox church and a synagogue
Assets: $7,451,945
Grant Range: $50,000 - $250

SNITE (FRED B.) FOUNDATION
4800 North Western Avenue
Chicago, IL 60625
Contact Person: Terrence J. Dillon, 550 Frontage Road, Northfield, IL 60093; (312) 446-7705
Geographic Giving Pattern: Primarily local

Special Interest: Roman Catholic church support and church-related educational institutions
Assets: $5,566,183
Grant Range: $39,815 - $100

SULLIVAN (BOLTON) FUND
One Northfield Plaza, Suite 310
Northfield, IL 60093
(312) 446-1500

Contact Person: Bolton Sullivan, President
Geographic Giving Pattern: National
Special Interest: Roman Catholic church support, secondary and higher education, church-related institutions and hospitals.
Assets: $2,004,273
Grant Range: $50,000 - $500
Limitation: No grants to individuals. Requests should be made by letter

WHITE (W.P. AND H.B.) FOUNDATION
540 Frontage Road, Suite 332
Northfield, IL 60093
(312) 446-1441

Contact Person: John H. McCortney, Vice-President
Geographic Giving Pattern: Primarily metropolitan Chicago
Special Interest: Roman Catholic church support, higher education, hospitals, church-related institutions
Assets: $12,825,545
Grant Range: $25,000 - $1,000

Louisiana

LIBBY-DUFOUR FUND
P.O. Box 61540
New Orleans, LA 70160
OR 321 Hibernia Bank Building, Suite 202
New Orleans, LA 70112
(504) 586-5552

Contact Person: James A. Stouse, President
Geographic Giving Pattern: Primarily local
Special Interest: Religious education
Assets: $4,902,372
Grant Range: $50,000 - $2,500
Limitation: No grants to individuals or for endowment funds

Maryland

KNOTT (MARION I. AND HENRY) FOUNDATION, INC., THE
Two West University Parkway
Baltimore, MD 21218
(301) 235-7068
Application address: 13008 Heil Manor Road, Route 1,
Reistertown, MD 21136
Contact Person: Margaret K. Riehl
Geographic Giving Pattern: Primarily local
Special Interest: Roman Catholic higher and secondary education, and
religious welfare organizations
Assets: $16,958,907
Grant Range: $100,000 - $35

MULLAN (THOMAS F. AND CLEMANTINE L.) FOUNDATION, INC., THE
15 Charles Plaza, Suite 400
Baltimore, MD 21201
(301) 727-6300
Contact Person: Thomas F. Mullan, Jr.
Geographic Giving Pattern: Primarily local
Special Interest: Church support, charitable institutions, higher and
secondary education
Assets: $3,259,400
Grant Range: $28,000 - $100
Limitation: Contributions made only to pre-selected charitable organizations

Massachusetts

BIRMINGHAM FOUNDATION
c/o Paul Mark Ryan
28 State Street, Suite 3780
Boston, MA 02109
(617) 723-7430
Contact Person: Paul Mark Ryan, Trustee
Geographic Giving Pattern: Primarily local
Special Interest: Roman Catholic charities, education and church support
Assets: $4,657,323
Grant Range: $40,000 - $1,000

WALSH (BLANCHE M.) CHARITABLE TRUST
c/o John E. Leggat
174 Central Street, Suite 329
Lowell, MA 01852
(617) 454-5654
Contact Person: Robert F. Murphy, Jr., Trustee
Geographic Giving Pattern: National
Special Interest: Roman Catholic charities and education
Assets: $1,905,905
Grant Range: $10,000 - $500

Michigan

SAGE FOUNDATION
2500 Comerci Building
Detroit, MI 48226
(313) 963-6420
Contact Person: Emmett E. Eagan, Sr., Vice-President
Geographic Giving Pattern: Primarily in Michigan
Special Interest: To further charitable, religious, scientific, literary and educational purposes
Assets: $32,887,85
Grant Range: $10,000 - $1,000

SEYMOUR AND TROESTER FOUNDATION
21500 Harper Avenue
St. Clair Shores, MI 48080
(313) 777-2775
Contact Person: B.A. Seymour, Jr., President
Geographic Giving Pattern: National
Special Interest: Roman Catholic charitable and religious organizations, higher and secondary educational institutions
Assets: $3,162,821
Grant Range: $47,000 - $500

TRACY (EMMET AND FRANCES) FUND
400 Renaissance Center, 35th Floor
Detroit, MI 48243
(313) 881-5007
Contact Person: Emmet E. Tracy, President
Geographic Giving Pattern: Primarily Michigan, some national
Special Interest: Roman Catholic religious organizations and missionary groups, hospitals, education

Assets: $866,098
Grant Range: $50,000 - $100

Minnesota

BUTLER (PATRICK AND AIMEE) FAMILY FOUNDATION
W-1380 First National Bank Building
St. Paul, MN 55101
(612) 222-2565
Contact Person: Sandra K. Butler
Geographic Giving Pattern: Primarily local
Special Interest: Roman Catholic church and related institutions
Assets: $5,269,640
Grant Range: $25,000 - $350
Limitation: No grants to individuals

KASAL (FATHER) CHARITABLE FUND
c/o Minnesota Trust Company
107 W. Oakland Avenue
Austin, MN 55912
(507) 437-3231
Contact Person: Warren F. Plunkett, President
Geographic Giving Pattern: International
Special Interest: Support for Roman Catholic charities in the United States
and for the education of young men and women for religious life, and
mission work
Assets: $1,632,400
Grant Range: $8,000 - $500

O'NEIL (CASEY ALBERT T.) FOUNDATION, THE
c/o First Trust Co. of St. Paul
W-555 First National Bank Building
St. Paul, MN 55101
(612) 291-5114
Contact Person: Jeffrey T. Peterson
Geographic Giving Pattern: Primarily local
Special Interest: Roman Catholic religious organizations and missions
Assets: $1,673,179
Grant Range: $30,000 - $1,000
Limitation: No grants to individuals

O'SHAUGHNESSY (I.A.) FOUNDATION
W-555 First National Bank Building
St. Paul, MN 55101
(612) 222-2323

Contact Person: Paul J. Kelly
Geographic Giving Pattern: Primarily Minnesota, Kansas, Texas and Illinois
Special Interest: Roman Catholic church-related institutions and church support
Assets: $21,324,792
Grant Range: $25,000 - 1,000 (Roman Catholic Giving)
Limitation: Grants normally initiated by foundation directors

QUINLAN (ELIZABETH C.) FOUNDATION, THE
417 Minnesota Federal Building
Minneapolis, MN 55402
(612) 333-8084

Contact Person: Richard A. Klein, President
Geographic Giving Pattern: Minnesota
Special Interest: Roman Catholic institutions
Assets: $1,865,520
Grant Range: $10,000 - $1,000 (Religious)

RAUENHORST (GERALD) FAMILY FOUNDATION
100 South Fifth Street
Minneapolis, MN 55402
(612) 342-2595

Contact Person: Michael P. Manning, Vice-President, Managing Director
Geographic Giving Pattern: Minnesota
Special Interest: General purpose contributions to well-established, religious, educational, and charitable organizations which are publicly supported
Assets: $6,451,250
Grant Range: $50,000 - $1,000 (Religious)
Limitation: Grants made only to pre-selected organizations. No unsolicited applications accepted

WASIE FOUNDATION, THE
909 Foshay Tower
Minneapolis, MN 55402
(612) 332-3883

Contact Person: David A. Odahowski, Executive Director
Geographic Giving Pattern: Limited to Minnesota, with emphasis on Minneapolis and St. Paul

Special Interest: Higher education, Roman Catholic religious associations
Assets: $11,419,032
Grant Range: $100,000 - $500

Missouri

ENRIGHT FOUNDATION, INC.
7508 Main
Kansas City, MO 64114
(816) 361-4942

Contact Person: Anna M. Cassidy
Geographic Giving Pattern: Primarily local
Special Interest: Roman Catholic religious organizations
Assets: $2,294,675
Grant Range: $20,000 - $100

SYCAMORE TREE TRUST
P.O. Box 11264
Clayton, MO 63105

Contact Person: R.J. Connors, Trustee
Geographic Giving Pattern: Missouri, New York
Special Interest: Roman Catholic church support and religious associations
Assets: $241,442
Grant Range: $11,500 - $200 (Religious)

VATTEROTT FOUNDATION
10449 St. Charles Rock Road
St. Ann, MO 63074
(314) 427-4000

Contact Person: Joseph H. Vatterott
Geographic Giving Pattern: Primarily local
Special Interest: Roman Catholic church support and church-related
institutions
Assets: $880,478
Grant Range: $18,000 - $100

New Jersey

ENGELHARD (CHARLES) FOUNDATION, THE
P.O. Box 427
Far Hills, NJ 07931
(201) 766-7224

Contact Person: Elaine Catterall, Secretary
Geographic Giving Pattern: National
Special Interest: Higher and secondary education, religious, cultural, medical and conservation organizations
Assets: $61,688,308
Grant Range: $20,000 - $3,000 (Denominational Giving)
Limitation: No grants to individuals

GRASSMANN (E.J.) TRUST
P.O. Box 4470
Watchung, NJ 07060
(201) 753-2440

Contact Person: William V. Engel, Executive Director
Geographic Giving Pattern: National
Special Interest: Hospitals, higher education and Roman Catholic church support
Assets: $25,969,790
Grant Range: $100,000 - $2,500

HACKETT FOUNDATION, INC., THE
2124 Oak Tree Road
Edison, NJ 08820
(201) 548-3686

Contact Person: Alice T. Hackett, Chair, Grant Committee
Special Interest: Roman Catholic religious orders and agencies relating to health and social services in the Northeast and foreign missions
Assets: $8,368,209
Grant Range: $25,000 - $1,000

KENNEDY (JOHN R.) FOUNDATION, INC., THE
75 Chestnut Ridge Road
Montvale, NJ 07645
(201) 391-1776

Contact Person: John R. Kennedy, Sr., President
Geographic Giving Pattern: New Jersey, New York, Washington, D.C.
Special Interest: Roman Catholic educatonial, religious and welfare programs
Assets: $6,599,175

New York

BRENCANDA FOUNDATION
358 Fifth Avenue, Suite 1103
New York, NY 10001

Contact Person: Peter S. Robinson, Executive Vice-President
Geographic Giving Pattern: United States and Canada
Special Interest: Roman Catholic religious organizations
Assets: $295,209
Grant Range: $51,325 - $5,000

GAISMAN (CATHERINE AND HENRY J.) FOUNDATION, THE
Box 277
Hartsdale, NY 10530
Contact Person: Catherine V. Gaisman, President
Geographic Giving Pattern: Primarily local
Special Interest: Roman Catholic church support
Assets: $3,994,568
Grant Range: $100,000 - $100

LA SALA (STEFANO) FOUNDATION, INC., THE
371 North Avenue
New Rochelle, NY 10801
(914) 235-1974
Contact Person: A. Stephan La Sala, Trustee
Geographic Giving Pattern: Primarily local
Special Interest: Chruch support, education, missions
Assets: $1,696.665
Grant Range: $11,000 - $50

HOMELAND FOUNDATION
c/o Kelley, Drye and Warren
101 Park Avenue
New York, NY 10178
(212) 808-7803
Contact Person: Chauncey Stillman, Trustee
Geographic Giving Pattern: National, international
Assets: $760,940
Grant Range: $20,000 - $500

HOPKINS (JOSEPHINE LAWRENCE) FOUNDATION
61 Broadway, Room 2912
New York, NY 10006
(212) 480-0400
Contact Person: Ivan Obolensky, President and Treasurer
Geographic Giving Pattern: Primarily local
Special Interest: Roman Catholic church support. Also hospitals and
medical research, community funds and cultural programs

Assets: $3,235,651
Grant Range: $20,000 - $1,000
Limitation: No grants to individuals

MASTRONARDI (CHARLES A.) FOUNDATION, THE
c/o Morgan Guaranty Trust Company
9 West 57th Street
New York, NY 10019
(212) 826-7603

Contact Person: Edward F. Bennett, Vice-President
Geographic Giving Pattern: Primarily New York and Florida
Special Interest: Higher education, child welfare, hospitals, Roman Catholic church support
Assets: $5,512,895
Grant Range: $85,000 - $500

MCCADDIN-MCQUIRK FOUNDATION, INC., THE
1002 Madison Avenue
New York, NY 10021
(212) 772-9090

Contact Person: Robert W. Dumser, Secretary
Geographic Giving Pattern: International
Special Interest: "Foster educational opportunities for poorer students to be priests, deacons, catechists or lay teachers of the Roman Catholic church. . . ."
Assets: $1,104,588
Grant Range: $2,000 - $600
Limitation: Application must be submitted by a Bishop, Rector, or head of a seminary

MCCARTHY CHARITIES, INC., THE
P.O. Box 576
Troy, NY 12181

Contact Person: James A. McCarthy, Vice-President
Geographic Giving Pattern: Primarily local, New York state capital district
Special Interest: Roman Catholic church support, church-related education and welfare agencies
Assets: $2,936,962
Grant Range: $9,000 - $500

MCCARTHY (MICHAEL W.) FOUNDATION, THE
One Liberty Plaza, 27th Floor
New York, NY 10006

Contact Person: Michael W. McCarthy, Manager
Geographic Giving Pattern: National
Special Interest: Higher education, church support and religious associations
Assets: $2,106,395
Grant Range: 20,000 - $100

MORANIA FOUNDATION, INC.
c/o Morgan Trust Company
9 West 57th Street
New York, NY 10019

Contact Person: Rev. Msgr. William J. McCormack, President; c/o Mr. Martin F. Shea, Sr. Vice-President, Morgan Guaranty Trust Co., 9 W. 57th Street, New York, NY 10019; (212) 286-7583
Geographic Giving Pattern: Primarily New York, some New England
Special Interest: Roman Catholic church-related institutions with emphasis on missions
Assets: $5,568,945
Grant Range: $175,000 - $2,000

O'NEIL (CYRIL F. AND MARIE E.) FOUNDATION
c/o Richards, O'Neil & Allegaert
660 Madison Avenue
New York, NY 10021
(212) 207-1200

Contact Person: Ralph M. O'Neil, President
Geographic Giving Pattern: Primarily local, some national
Special Interest: Education and Catholic religious organizations
Assets: $1,983,738
Grant Range: $125,000 - $100

O'TOOLE (THERESA AND EDWARD) FOUNDATION
c/o The Bank of New York
48 Wall Street
New York, NY 10015

Contact Person: William Wiseman, Trust officer
Special Interest: Roman Catholic welfare and educational funds
Assets: $14,143,682
Grant Range: $80,000 - $1,000 (Denominational Giving)

POPE FOUNDATION, THE
211 W. 56th Street
New York, NY 10019

Contact Person: Fortune Pope, Vice-President
Geographic Giving Pattern: Primarily local, some national and international

Special Interest: Education, religion, relief and rehabilitation, hospitals, and medical research. Also civic organizations
Assets: $16,299,320
Grant Range: $25,000 -$500 (Religious)

REISS (JACOB L.) FOUNDATION
c/o Irving Trust Company
P.O. Box 12446
Church Street Station
New York, NY 10249

Contact Person: Irving Trust Co., Trustee
Geographic Giving Pattern: Primarily New York, New Jersey, Wisconsin
Special Interest: Hospitals, Roman Catholic educational and welfare organizations
Assets: $2,154,633
Grant Range: $44,000 - $1,000
Limitation: No grants to individuals

SAYOUR (ELIAS) FOUNDATION, INC.
185 Madison Avenue
New York, NY 10016
(212) 686-7560

Contact Person: Jeanette Sayour, President
Geographic Giving Pattern: Primarily local
Special Interest: Roman Catholic church support, welfare funds, educational and religious organizations
Assets: $1,137,643
Grant Range: $5,300 - $50

North Carolina

BRYAN (KATHLEEN PRICE AND JOSEPH M.) FAMILY FOUNDATION, THE
P.O.Box 1349
Greensboro, NC 27402
(919) 275-7275

Geographic Giving Pattern: Primarily North Carolina
Special Interest: Religious and educational iNStitutions
Assets: $1,567,420
Grant Range: $10,000 - $1,000

Ohio

BENTZ FOUNDATION
2569 Berwick Blvd.
Columbus, OH 43209
(614) 239-0920

Contact Person: George B. Bentz, President
Geographic Giving Pattern: National, international
Special Interest: Missions, church support
Assets: $1,696,279
Grant Range: $100,000 - $500
Limitation: No unsolicited applications accepted

KUNTZ FOUNDATION
120 West Second Street
Dayton, OH 45402
(513) 461-3870

Contact Person: Peter H. Kuntz, President
Geographic Giving Pattern: Primarily local
Special Interest: Higher education, hospitals, community funds, Roman Catholic church and missions support
Assets: $2,148,973
Grant Range: $25,000 - $50

LENNON (FRED A.) FOUNDATION
29500 Solon Road
Solon, OH 44139
(216) 248-4600

Contact Person: John F. Fant, Jr., Secretary
Geographic Giving Pattern: Primarily local
Special Interest: Higher education, hospitals, public policy, Roman Catholic church support
Assets: $8,584,843
Grant Range: $130,000 - $100

O'NEIL (W.) FOUNDATION, THE
One General Street
Akron, OH 44329
(216) 666-6006

Contact Person: Miss Flora Flint, Vice President, Secretary-Treasurer
Geographic Giving Pattern: National
Special Interest: Roman Catholic church support and church-related institutions

Assets: $12,384,176
Grant Range: $500,000 - $900

O'NEIL BROTHERS FOUNDATION, THE
23200 Chagrin Blvd.
Cleveland, OH 44122
(216) 464-2121

Contact Person: Patrick O'Neil, President
Geographic Giving Pattern: Cleveland, Ohio and Florida
Special Interest: Roman Catholic religious organizations and church support
Assets: $113, 931 (M) + $50,229 (Contributions, gifts, etc.)
Grant Range: $3,000 - $100

WASMER (JOHN C.) FOUNDATION, THE
13001 Athens Avenue
Lakewood, OH 44107

Contact Person: Florence M. Wasner, Manager
Geographic Giving Pattern: Primarily Cleveland, OH
Special Interest: Roman Catholic organizations
Assets: $558,191 (M) & $326,667 (Contributions, gifts, etc.)
Grant Range: $25,000 - $25

Oklahoma

WARREN (WILLIAM K.) FOUNDATION, THE
P.O. Box 45372
Tulsa, OK 74145
(928) 492-8100

Contact Person: Mr. W.R. Lissau
Geographic Giving Pattern: National
Special Interest: Church support, Roman Catholic religious associations, local medical research centers and hospitals
Assets: $114,961,112
Grant Range: $156,000 - $100 (Religious)
Limitation: Grant funds are presently committed

Oregon

CLARK FOUNDATION
255 S.W. Harrison Street, GA 2
Portland, OR 97201
(503) 223-5290

Contact Person: Maurie D. Clark, President
Geographic Giving Pattern: Oregon
Special Interest: Roman Catholic educational, religious, charitable, medical organizations
Assets: $74,037 (M) plus $288,393 (Gifts, etc.)
Grant Range: $10,000 - $500 (Religious)

FRANK (A.J.) FAMILY FOUNDATION
P.O. Drawer 79
Mill City, OR 97360

Contact Person: A.J. Frank, President
Geographic Giving Pattern: Primarily local
Special Interest: Roman Catholic church support and welfare funds
Assets: $1,855,703
Grant Range: $40,000 - $500

JOHN (B.P.) FOUNDATION
1404 Standard Plaza
Portland, OR 97204

Contact Person: Lester M. John, President, Treasurer
Geographic Giving Pattern: National, international
Special Interest: Roman Catholic religious, charitable and educational organizations
Assets: $1,254,330
Grant Range: $10,000 - $500

JOHN (HELEN) FOUNDATION
1404 Standard Plaza
Portland, OR 97204

Contact Person: James G. Condon, President
Geographic Giving Pattern: Primarily local
Special Interest: Roman Catholic religious, charitable, educational purposes
Assets: $1,224,344
Grant Range: $8,000 - $500

Pennsylvania

CONNELLY FOUNDATION
9300 Ashton Road
Philadelphia, PA 19136
(215) 698-5203

Contact Person: Mrs. Rowena M. Zurybida, Exec. Asst. to the Director
Geographic Giving Pattern: Primarily Philadelphia area
Special Interest: Religious and educational institutions and hospitals

Assets: $75,442,247
Grant Range: $111,250 - $100 (Religious)
Limitation: No grants to individuals or for endowment funds

DONNELLY (MARY J.) FOUNDATION
c/o Thomas J. Donnelly
2510 Centre City Tower
Pittsburgh, PA 15222
(412) 471-5828

Contact Person: Thomas J. Donnelly, Trustee
Geographic Giving Pattern: Primarily local, some New York, West
Virginia, North Carolina, Washington, D.C. and Connecticut
Special Interest: Roman Catholic educational, welfare, and religious
organizations

Assets: $2,236,978
Grant Range: $17,000 - $1,000
Limitation: Contributions to pre-selected organizations

KELLEY (KATE M.) FOUNDATION
301 Meade Street
Pittsburgh, PA 15221
(412) 243-3080

Contact Person: Edward C. Ifft, Trustee
Geographic Giving Pattern: National
Special Interest: Roman Catholic church, education, welfare support
Assets: $4,434,698
Grant Range: $10,000 - $1,000

MCSHAIN (JOHN) CHARITIES
540 N. 17th Street
Philadelphia, PA 19130
(215) 564-2322

Contact Person: John McShain, President
Geographic Giving Pattern: Primarily local
Special Interest: Roman Catholic religious, educational and welfare pur-
poses

Assets: $36,064,631
Grant Range: $100,500 - $10 (Roman Catholic Giving)
Limitation: No grants to individuals

ST. MARYS CATHOLIC FOUNDATION
1935 State Street
St. Marys, PA 15857

Contact Person: Richard J. Reuscher, Secretary-Treasurer
Geographic Giving Pattern: Pennsylvania, New Jersey, Indiana, New York, Washington, D.C.
Special Interest: Roman Catholic schools - all levels. Also religious associations
Assets: $3,015,004
Grant Range: $104,500 - $5,000
Limitation: No grants to individuals or for endowment funds

Texas

BURKITT FOUNDATION, THE
2000 West Loop South, Suite 1485
Houston, TX 77027
(713) 439-0149
Contact Person: Joseph W. Ryan, Vice President
Geographic Giving Pattern: Primarily local, some national, international
Special Interest: Roman Catholic church-sponsored programs
Assets: $8,511,508
Grant Range: $25,000 - $500

CAMERON (HARRY S. AND ISABEL C.) FOUNDATION
P.O. Box 2555
Houston, TX 77001
(713) 652-6526
Contact Person: Carl W. Schumacher, Jr.
Geographic Giving Pattern: Primarily local, some national
Special Interest: Roman Catholic churches, schools - all levels, and religious organizations
Assets: $11,239,305
Grant Range: $40,000 - $500 (Roman Catholic Giving)
Limitation: No grants to individuals

DOUGHERTY (JAMES R.), JR. FOUNDATION, THE
P.O. Box 640
Beeville, TX 78104-0640
(512) 358-3560
Contact Person: Hugh Grove, Jr., Assistant Secretary
Geographic Giving Pattern: Primarily local
Special Interest: Roman Catholic church-related institutions
Assets: $8,068,383
Grant Range: $50,000 - $5,000 (Roman Catholic Giving)
Limitation: No grants to individuals

HENCK (AUGUST J. AND SADIE L.) MEMORIAL FUND
P.O. Box 1237
Austin, TX 78767
(512) 477-9831
Contact Person: Henck Memorial Fund Trustees
Geographic Giving Pattern: Primarily Texas
Special Interest: Roman Catholic organizations
Assets: $1,687,457
Grant Range: $25,000 - $3,000 (Religious)

KENEDY (JOHN G. AND MARIE STELLA) MEMORIAL
FOUNDATION, THE
1020 First City Tower II
Corpus Christi, TX 78478
Contact Person: James R. McCown
Geographic Giving Pattern: Limited to Texas
Assets: $98,340,219
Grant Range: $800,000 - $15,000

STRAKE FOUNDATION
712 Main Street, Suite 3300
Houston, TX 77002-3210
(713) 546-2400
Contact Person: George W. Strake, Jr., President
Geographic Giving Pattern: National, with emphasis on Texas
Special Interest: Public charitable, religious, educational, scientific and/or
literary purposes for the public good
Assets: $13,588,695
Grant Range: $10,000 - $500 (Denominational Giving)
Limitation: No grants to individuals

Washington

NORCLIFFE FUND, THE
999 Third Avenue, Suite 1515
Seattle, WA 98104
(206) 682-4820
Contact Person: Mary Ellen Hughes, President
Geographic Giving Pattern: Pacific Northwest
Special Interest: Church support, religious associations, education,
youth, aged
Assets: $8,864,851
Grant Range: $11,000 - $65 (Religious)

Wisconsin

DE RANCE, INC.
7700 West Blue Mound Road
Milwaukee, WI 53213
(414) 475-7700

Contact Person: Idella J. Gallagher, Senior Vice-President
Geographic Giving Pattern: National, international
Special Interest: Roman Catholic church support, religious associations, missionary work, welfare
Assets: $110,106,434
Grant Range: $250,000 - $500
Limitation: No grants to individuals or for endowment funds

Jewish Foundations

California

AMADO (MAURICE) FOUNDATION
1800 Century Park East, Suite 200
Los Angeles, CA 90067
(213) 556-0116

Contact Person: Richard J. Amado, President
Special Interest: Sephardic Jewish causes
Assets: $9,578,194
Grant Range: $55,000 - $160

FRIEDMAN BROTHERS FOUNDATION
801 E. Commercial Street
Los Angeles, CA 90012

Contact Person: Leslie Mendelsohn; 109 N. Highland, Los Angeles, CA 90036
Geographic Giving Pattern: Primarily local
Special Interest: Education, including religious education and Jewish welfare funds
Assets: $2,583,696
Grant Range: $18,500 - $250

HAAS (WALTER AND ELISE) FUND
1155 Battery Street
San Francisco, CA 94111
(415) 398-4474

Contact Person: Bruce R. Sievers, Executive Director; 1090 Sansome Street, San Francisco, CA 94111
Geographic Giving Pattern: Israel and California
Special Interest: Jewish religious purposes
Assets: $48,253,595
Grant Range: $250,000 - $500

LEVY (HYMAN JEBB) FOUNDATION
2222 S. Figueroa Street
Los Angeles, CA 90007
(213) 749-9441

Contact Person: Hyman J. Levy, President
Geographic Giving Pattern: United States and Israel
Special Interest: Jewish education and temple support
Assets: $2,909,804
Grant Range: $48,500 - $750

SHAPELL (DAVID AND FELA) FOUNDATION
9401 Wilshire Boulevard, Suite 1200
Beverly Hills, CA 90212
(213) 273-7337
Contact Person: David Shapell, President
Geographic Giving Pattern: California, New York and Israel
Special Interest: Jewish welfare funds, temple support, religious education
Assets: $725,668
Grant Range: $12,000 - $50

WEINBERG (ADOLPH AND ETTA) FOUNDATION
12948 S. Pioneer Boulevard
P.O. Box 723
Norwalk, CA 90650
(213) 864-2781
Contact Person: Ray Molene; P.O. Box 1022, Norwalk, CA 90651-1022
Geographic Giving Pattern: Primarily local
Special Interest: Jewish religious organizations and temple support
Assets: $1,618,582
Grant Range: $80,000 - $15

Colorado

COORS (ADOLPH) FOUNDATION
350-C Clayton Street
Denver, CO 80206
(303) 388-1636
Contact Person: Linda S. Tafoya, Executive Manager
Geographic Giving Pattern: Primarily Colorado
Special Interest: To support religious, charitable and educational organizations - Jewish or Christian
Assets: $87,659,836
Grant Range: $10,000 - $1,000 (Denominational Giving)

Delaware

KUTZ (MILTON AND HATTIE) FOUNDATION
101 Garden of Eden Road
Wilmington, DE 19803
(302) 478-6200
Contact Person: Executive Director, Jewish Federation of Delaware
Geographic Giving Pattern: Local
Special Interest: Jewish religious organizations and temple support

Assets: $1,817,391
Grant Range: $20,000 - $500

District of Columbia

GUDELSKY (ISADORE AND BERTHA) FAMILY FOUNDATION, INC., THE
c/o Philip Margolius
1503 21st Street, N.W.
Washington, D.C. 20036
(202) 328-0500
Contact Person: Philip Margolius
Geographic Giving Pattern: Primarily local
Special Interest: Jewish welfare funds and temple support
Assets: $7,132,367

Florida

APPLEBAUM FOUNDATION, INC., THE
4925 Collins Avenue
Miami Beach, FL 33140
(305) 651-6478

Contact Person: Joseph Applebaum
Geographic Giving Pattern: General
Special Interest: Higher education, hospitals, medical research, Jewish welfare agencies, religious schools and temple support
Assets: $3,782,309
Grant Range: $30,000 - $1,000

BLANK (SAMUEL AND FAMILY) FOUNDATION
8940 N.W. 24th Terrace
Miami, FL 33172
(305) 591-3582

Contact Person: Marvin Florman; 8940 N.W. 24th Terrace
Geographic Giving Pattern: Primarily local
Special Interest: Jewish welfare funds, hospitals, educaiton, temple support
Assets: $4,110,587
Grant Range: $72,000 - $250

Illinois

PRITZKER FOUNDATION
2 First National Plaza, 30th Floor
Chicao, IL 60603
(312) 621-4200

Contact Person: Simon Zunaman
Geographic Giving Pattern: National
Special Interest: Higher education, religious welfare funds and temple support
Assets: $4,799,791
Limitation: No grants to individuals. Funds fully committed; applications not accepted

SHAPIRO (CHARLES AND M.R.) FOUNDATION, INC.
330 W. Diversey Parkway #1801
Chicago, IL 60657
Contact Person: Morris R. Shapiro, President
Geographic Giving Pattern: Primarily local
Special Interest: Jewish welfare funds. Also contributions to Catholic and Protestant churches
Assets: $13,090,644
Grant Range: $125,000 - $25
Limitation: No grants to individuals

Iowa

ALIBIR FOUNDATION
1200 Carriers Building
Des Moines, IA 50309
(515) 288-9723
Contact Person: Philip Burns, Treasurer
Geographic Giving Pattern: Primarily local
Special Interest: Higher education, Jewish welfare funds, and temple support
Assets: $1,513,868
Grant Range: $125,000 - $4,000

Maryland

CHERTKOF (DAVID W. AND ANNIE) MITZVAH FUND, INC.
19 W. Franklin Street
Baltimore, MD 21201
(301) 727-5155
Contact Person: Howard L. Chertkof, Secretary
Geographic Giving Pattern: Maryland, New York and Florida
Special Interest: Jewish sponsored educational programs, temples, welfare funds
Assets: $841,479
Grant Range: $17,000 - $45

MENDELSON (ALFRED G. AND IDA) FAMILY FOUNDATION
8300 Pennsylvania Avenue
P.O. Box 398
Forestville, MD 20747-0398
(301) 420-6400
Contact Person: Ida Mendelson, President
Geographic Giving Pattern: Primarily local
Special Interest: Jewish religious organizations. Also community, social services, and educational funds
Assets: $161,964
Grant Range: $37,062 - $100 (Religious)

WASSERMAN (GEORGE) FOUNDATION, INC.
5454 Wisconsin Avenue, Suite 1300
Chevy Chase, MD 20815
(301) 657-4222
Contact Person: Louis C. Grossberg, President and Treasurer
Geographic Giving Pattern: International
Special Interest: Jewish welfare funds, theological studies, temple support
Assets: $2,779,195
Grant Range: $58,000 - $100

WEINBERG (HARRY AND JEANETTE) FOUNDATION, INC., THE
5518 Baltimore National Pike
Baltimore, MD 21228
(301) 744-6142
Contact Person: Nathan Weinberg, Vice-President and Secretary
Geographic Giving Pattern: Hawaii, Baltimore, Scranton, Pennsylvania
Special Interest: Jewish welfare funds, temple support, higher education
Assets: $10,269,836
Grant Range: $150,000 - $10
Limitation: Grants made only to pre-selected charitable organizations. Unsolicited applications not accepted

Massachusetts

STONE CHARITABLE FOUNDATION, INC., THE
P.O. Box 728
Wareham, MA 02571
(6517) 759-3503
Contact Person: Stephen A. Stone, President
Geographic Giving Pattern: Primarily in Massachusetts
Special Interest: Jewish welfare, higher education

Assets: $4,319,517
Grant Range: $155,000 - $25
Limitation: No grants to individuals

Michigan

BARGMAN (THEODORE AND MINA) FOUNDATION
29201 Telegraph Road, Suite 500
Southfield, MI 48034
(313) 353-9500

Contact Person: Joseph H. Jackier, President
Geographic Giving Pattern: National, international
Special Interest: Primarily religious giving with emphasis on Jewish welfare funds, higher education in Israel, temple support
Assets: $3,073,977
Grant Range: $41,000 - $200
Limitation: Contributions to pre-selected organizations only. No unsolicited applications accepted

HERMAN (JOHN AND ROSE) FOUNDATION
3001 W. Big Beaver Pond, Suite 404
Troy, MI 48084
(313) 649-6400

Contact Person: Harold S. Tobias, Secretary
Geographic Giving Pattern: Primarily local
Special Interest: Jewish welfare funds and temple support
Assets: $1,695,134
Grant Range: $16,000 - $100

PRENTIS (MEYER AND ANNA) FAMILY FOUNDATION, INC., THE
14500 W. Seven Mile Road
Detroit, MI 48235
(313) 342-7100

Contact Person: Lester Morris, Secretary
Geographic Giving Pattern: National
Special Interest: Temple support, education, health and welfare organizations
Assets: $8,649,562
Grant Range: $160,000 - $100

STOLLMAN FOUNDATION, THE
2900 W. Maple Road
Troy, MI 48084
(313) 643-6140

Contact Person: Max Stollman, President
Geographic Giving Pattern: New York, Michigan and Israel
Special Interest: Religious education, temple support, welfare funds
Assets: $239,587
Grant Range: $30,000 - $500

Minnesota

PHILLIPS FOUNDATION, THE
100 Washington Square, Suite 1650
Minneapolis, MN 55401
(612) 331-6230
Contact Person: Thomas P. Cook, Executive Director; The Phillips Foun-
dation, 235 N.E. Kennedy Street, Minneapolis, MN 55415
Geographic Giving Pattern: Primarily mid-west
Special Interest: Higher education including medical and theological,
Jewish welfare and temple support
Assets: $42,246,035
Grant Range: $3,000 - $100 (Religious)
Limitation: No grants to individuals or for endowment funds

Nebraska

LIVINGSTON (MILTON S. AND CORINNE N.) FOUNDATION, INC., THE
300 Overland Wolf Center
6910 Pacific Street
Omaha, NE 68106
(402) 558-1112
Contact Person: Yale Richards, Secretary
Geographic Giving Pattern: Primarily local
Special Interest: Jewish welfare funds, higher education, temple support
Assets: $2,692,489
Grant Range: $100,000 - $2,500 (Religious)
Limitation: No grants to individuals

New Jersey

FRISCH FOUNDATION, INC., THE
1600 Parker Avenue
Fort Lee, NJ 07024
(212 324-0300
Mailing Address: 501 East 79th Street, New York, NY 10021

Contact Person: Alfred M. Frisch, President
Geographic Giving Pattern: United States and Israel
Special Interest: Jewish welfare funds, temple support. Also higher education, women's organizations and hospitals
Assets: $1,355,745
Grant Range: $50,000 - $100

ROSENHAUS (SARAH ADN MATTHEW) PEACE FOUNDATION, INC., THE
Picatinny Road
Morristown, NJ 07960
(201) 267-6583
Contact Person: Irving Rosenhaus, Director
Geographic Giving Pattern: Primarily New Jersey and New York, also Israel
Special Interest: To promote world peace and understanding. Grants to higher education including theological. Also to Jewish welfare funds and temple support
Assets: $8,611,103
Grant Range: $145,000 - $520 (Religious & Welfare)

New York

ADES FOUNDATION, INC.
17 E. 37th Street
New York , NY 10016
Contact Person: Joseph Ades, President
Geographic Giving Pattern: New York and Israel
Special Interest: Jewish welfare, temple support,education
Assets: $307,675
Grant Range: $100,000 - $25

BENDHEIM (CHARLES AND ELS) FOUNDATION
10 Columbus Circle
New York, NY 10019
Contact Person: Charles H. Bendheim, President
Geographic Giving Pattern: National
Special Interest: Jewish-sponsored religious and educational institutions and welfare funds
Assets: $365,020
Grant Range: $25,000 - $10

BRAND (MARTHA AND REGINA) FOUNDATION, INC., THE
521 Fifth Avenue
New York, NY 10175
(212) 687-3505

Contact Person: Nathan B. Kogan, President
Geographic Giving Pattern: Primarily local
Special Interest: Jewish welfare funds, temple support, and a theological seminary
Assets: $1,509,614
Grant Range: $30,000 - $50

DANIEL (GERARD AND RUTH) FOUNDATION, INC.
5 Plain Avenue
New Rochelle, NY 10801
(914) 235-2525

Contact Person: Gerard Daniel, President
Geographic Giving Pattern: Primarily local
Special Interest: Jewish religious and welfare funds
Assets: $2,238,153
Grant Range: $46,000 - $150 (Religious)

DAVIS (SIMON AND ANNA) FOUNDATION
c/o Davis & Gilbert
850 Third Avenue
New York, NY 10022
(212) 593-0707

Contact Person: Paul B. Gibney, Jr., President and Treasurer
Geographic Giving Pattern: Primarily local
Special Interest: Religious welfare funds, higher education in the United States and Israel
Assets: $2,532,112
Grant Range: $35,500 - $2,000

HASENFELD (A. AND Z.) FOUNDATION, INC.
580 Fifth Avenue
New York, NY 10036

Contact Person: Alexander Hasenfeld, President
Special Interest: Jewish welfare funds, temple support
Assets: $27,116 plus $104,179 (Gifts, etc.)
Grant Range: $13,716 - $10

HESS FOUNDATION,INC.
1185 Avenue of the Americas
New York, NY 10036
(212) 997-8500

Contact Person: Leon Hess, President
Geographic Giving Pattern: National
Special Interest: A disaster relief fund, education, temple and church support

Assets: $66,422,290
Grant Range: $55,000 - $500 (Religious)

JESSELSON FOUNDATION
1221 Avenue of the Americas
New York, NY 10020
Contact Person: Ludwig Jesselson, President and Treasurer
Geographic Giving Pattern: International
Special Interest: Temple support, Jewish welfare funds, Jewish-sponsored educational and charitable institutions
Assets: $22,295,195
Grant Range: $110,675 - $15

MORGANSTERN (MORRIS) FOUNDATION
100 Merrick Road
Rockville Center, NY 11570
(516) 536-3030
Contact Person: Hannah Klein, Executive Director
Geographic Giving Pattern: Primarily New York area
Special Interest: Jewish welfare funds, religious institutions, particularly synagogues
Assets: $10,013,691
Grant Range: $370,000 - $25

OVERSEAS FOUNDATIONS, INC.
511 Fifth Avenue
New York, NY 10017
(212) 573-1845
Contact Person: Morton P. Hyman, Manager
Geographic Giving Pattern: National, primarily New York, also Israel
Special Interest: Charitable, educational, religious
Assets: $965,225
Grant Range: $25,000 - $50
Limitation: No unsolicited applications accepted

RAMAPO TRUST
126 E. 56th Street
New York, NY 10022
(212) 308-7355
Contact Person: Stephen L. Schwartz, Manager
Geographic Giving Pattern: Primarily New York, New Jersey
Special Interest: Charitable, religious, educational purposes
Assets: $36,591,478
Grant Range: $744,444 - $1,000
Limitation: No grants to individuals. Unsolicited proposals not accepted

RIDGEFIELD FOUNDATION, THE
820 Second Avenue
New York, NY 10017
(212) 692-9570

Contact Person: Mrs. Marguerite M. Riposanu, Treasurer
Geographic Giving Pattern: National, also Israel
Special Interest: Charitable, religious, educational purposes
Assets: $2,053,628
Grant Range: $5,000 - $100
Limitation: No grants to individuals

STEIN (JOSEPH F.) FOUNDATION, INC.
28 Aspen Road
Scarsdale, NY 10583
(914) 725-1770

Contact Person: Melvin M. Stein, Manager
Geographic Giving Pattern: Primarily local
Special Interest: Religious education and Jewish welfare
Assets: $4,225,764
Grant Range: $98,400 - $25

STERN (JEROME L. AND JANE) FOUNDATION, INC.
745 Fifth Avenue
New York, NY 10022

Contact Person: Jerome L. Stern, Chairman
Geographic Giving Pattern: Primarily local
Special Interest: Jewish religious education, temple support and Jewish welfare funds
Assets: $2,088,905
Grant Range: $25,000 - $25

TANANBAUM (MARTIN) FOUNDATION, INC.
261 Madison Avenue, 16th Floor
New York, NY 10017
(212) 687-3440

Contact Person: Arnold S. Alperstein, Manager
Geographic Giving Pattern: National
Special Interest: Religious education, temple support, welfare
Assets: $2,015,663
Grant Range: $29,500 - $50
Limitation: No grants to individuals

TUDOR FOUNDATION, INC.
551 Fifth Avenue
New York, NY 10176
(212) 682-8490
Contact Person: Edwin A. Malloy, Treasurer
Geographic Giving Pattern: National
Special Interest: "To promote a better understanding among peoples of all races, creeds and backgrounds." Grants to institutions promoting this purpose. Support also for Jewish theological education and welfare
Assets: $3,686,985
Grant Range: $20,000 - $500
Limitation: No grants to individuals

WOLFKOWSKI FOUNDATION, INC.
One State Street Plaza
New York, NY 10004
Contact Person: Abraham Wolfson, Manager
Geographic Giving Pattern: United States and Israel
Special Interest: Jewish religious education, temple support and welfare funds
Assets: $115,022
Grant Range: $16,500 - $100

Ohio

MELTON (SAMUEL MENDEL) FOUNDATION
17 South High Street
Columbus, OH 43215
(614) 224-5239
Contact Person: Samuel M. Melton
Geographic Giving Pattern: United States and Israel
Special Interest: Higher education and youth agencies in Israel and Jewish religious educational organizations
Assets: $1,050,015
Grant Range: $232,550 - $50

SAPIRSTEIN (JACOB) FOUNDATION OF CLEVELAND, THE
10500 American Road
Cleveland, OH 44144
(216) 525-7300
Contact Person: Irving R. Stone, President
Geographic Giving Pattern: National
Special Interest: Jewish welfare funds, secondary and higher religious education

Assets: $16,216,467
Grant Range: $106,310 - $100
Limitation: No grants to individuals

Pennsylvania

HYMAN FAMILY FOUNDATION
6315 Forbes Avenue
Pittsburgh, PA 15217
(412) 521-1000

Contact Person: Mrs. Yetta Elinoff, Manager
Geographic Giving Pattern: Primarily local
Special Interest: Temple support, religious education, welfare
Assets: $1,577,999
Grant Range: $15,000 - $100

KLINE (CHARLES AND FIGA) FOUNDATION
302 Colonial Building
Allentown, PA 18101
(215) 434-6149

Contact Person: Leonard Rapoport, Director
Geographic Giving Pattern: Primarily local
Special Interest: Temple support and Jewish welfare agencies
Assets: $5,531,815
Grant Range: $171,000 - $500
Limitation: No grants to individuals

MILLSTEIN CHARITABLE FOUNDATION, THE
N. 4th Street & Gaskill Avenue
Jeanette, PA 15644
(412) 523-5531

Contact Person: David J. Millstein, Executive Secretary
Special Interest: Jewish welfare funds, temple support
Assets: $1,634,434
Grant Range: $25,000 - $10

STEINSAPIR (JULIUS L. AND LIBBIE B.) FAMILY FOUNDATION
900 Lawyers Building
Pittsburgh, PA 15219
(412) 391-2920

Contact Person: Samuel Horovitz, Trustee
Geographic Giving Pattern: Primarily local
Special Interest: Temple support, Jewish welfare funds, education

Assets: $1,658,269
Grant Range: $20,000 - $100

Rhode Island

HASSENFELD FOUNDATION, THE
1027 Newport Avenue
Pawtucket, RI 02861
(401) 726-4100
Contact Person: Stephen Hassenfeld, Secretary-Treasurer
Geographic Giving Pattern: Rhode Island and Jerusalem
Special Interest: Jewish welfare funds, religious organizations, education
Assets: $893,386
Grant Range: $150,000 - $74,950

Tennessee

BELZ FOUNDATION
5118 Park Avenue
Memphis, TN 38117
(901) 767-4780
Contact Person: Jack A. Belz, Manager
Geographic Giving Pattern: Primarily local
Special Interest: Jewish welfare funds, temple support, education
Assets: $3,704,748
Grant Range: $6,000 - $18 (Religious)
Limitation: No grants to individuals

GOLDSMITH FOUNDATION, INC.
123 S. Main Street
P.O. Box 449
Memphis, TN 38143
(901) 529-4716
Contact Person: Jack L. Goldsmith, President
Geographic Giving Pattern: Primarily local, some national
Special Interest: Charitable, medical, educational, religious including temple support
Assets: $2,934,037
Grant Range: $67,500 - $100

Wisconsin

KOHL (ALLEN D.) CHARITABLE FOUNDATION, INC.
4300 W. Brown Deer Road, Suite 120
Milwaukee, WI 53223
(414) 354-6550

Contact Person: Allen D. Kohl, President
Geographic Giving Pattern: Primarily local
Special Interest: Jewish welfare and temple support
Assets: $4,835,690
Grant Range: $45,000 - $100

Interfaith Foundations

California

HERBST FOUNDATION, INC. THE
4 Embarcadero Center
San Francisco, CA 94111
(415) 627-8384

Contact Person: John T. Seigle, Manager
Geographic Giving Pattern: Primarily local
Special Interest: Educational and religious organizations
Religious Preference: Protestant, Roman Catholic, Jewish
Assets: $32,245,461
Grant Range: $335,000 - $500; $20,000 - $1,000 (Grant Average)

IRVINE (JAMES) FOUNDATION, THE
One Market Plaza
Steuart Street Tower, Suite 2305
San Francisco, CA 94105
(415) 777-2244

Contact Person: Luz A. Vega, Program Director
Southern CA Grant Application Office: 450 Newport Center Drive, Suite 545, Newport Beach, CA 92660; (714) 644-1362
Contact Person: Doris C. Jones, Asst. Vice-President
Geographic Giving Pattern: Limited to California
Assets: $309,977,723
Grant Range: $1,000,000 - $1,500
Limitation: No grants to individuals

JEWETT (GEORGE FREDERICK) FOUNDATION
One Maritime Plaza
The Alcoa Building, Suite 1340
San Francisco, CA 94111
(415) 421-1351

Contact Person: Sara C. Fernandez, Program Director
Geographic Giving Pattern: Primarily Pacific Northwest
Special Interest: Religious training
Religious Preference: Protestant, Roman Catholic
Assets: $16,300,000
Grant Range: $50,000 - $500

District of Columbia

CAFRITZ (MORRIS AND GWENDOLYN) FOUNDATION, THE
1825 K Street, N.W.
Washington, D.C. 20006
(202) 862-6800

Contact Person: Martin Atlas, Vice President
Geographic Giving Pattern: District of Columbia, only to programs of direct assistance to the District
Assets: $153,013,338
Grant Range: $100,000 - $1,000
Limitation: No grants to individuals

MCGREGOR (THOMAS AND FRANCES) FOUNDATION
c/o Robert Philipson & Co.
2000 L Street, N.W., Suite 609
Washington, D.C. 20036

Contact Person: Victor Krakower; 2121 K Street, N.W., Washington, D.C. 20037; (202) 333-4411
Geographic Giving Pattern: Primarily local
Special Interest: Education, hospitals, health agencies, cultural programs and religious organizations
Religious Preference: Jewish, Roman Catholic, Protestant
Assets: $2,856,753
Grant Range: $15,000 - $50

MEYER (EUGENE AND AGNES E.) FOUNDATION
1200 15th Street, N.W., Suite 500
Washington, D.C. 20005
(202) 659-2435

Contact Person: Kathy L. Dwyer, Program Officer
Geographic Giving Pattern: Primarily in the Washington D.C. metropolitan area
Assets: $32,833,330
Grant Range: $33,750 - $100

Florida

DAVIS (ARTHUR VINING) FOUNDATIONS, THE
Haskell Building, Suite 520
Oak & Fisk Streets
Jacksonville, FL 32204
(904) 359-0670

Contact Person: Dr. Max K. Morris, Executive Director
Geographic Giving Pattern: National
Special Interest: Theological seminaries, campus ministry
Religious Preference: Protestant, Roman Catholic, Jewish
Assets: $69,902,000
Grant Range: $247,000 - $2,000

JENKINS (GEORGE W.) FOUNDATION, INC.
P.O. Box 407
Lakeland, FL 33802
(813) 688-1188

Contact Person: George W. Jenkins, President
Geographic Giving Pattern: Primarily local
Special Interest: Church support
Religious Preference: Protestant, Roman Catholic, Jewish
Assets: $5,560,377
Grant Range: $10,000 - $100 (Religious)
Limitation: No grants to individuals. Applications from organizations outside of Florida will not be considered

Georgia

WHITEHEAD (JOSEPH B.) FOUNDATION
1400 Peachtree Center Tower
230 Peachtree Street, N.W.
Atlanta, GA 30303
(404) 522-6755

Contact Person: Boisfeuillet Jones, President
Geographic Giving Pattern: Limited to Atlanta, GA
Special Interest: Child/Youth welfare, also elderly and indigent
Assets: $81,184,569
Grant Range: $50,000 - $1,000

Illinois

RETIREMENT RESEARCH FOUNDATION
325 Toughy Avenue
Parl Ridge, IL 60068
(312) 823-4133

Contact Person: Marilyn Hennessy, Executive Director
Geographic Giving Pattern: National
Special Interest: To improve the quality of life of older persons in the U.S.

Assets: $70,831,537
Grant Range: $45,000 - $4,062 (Religious Institutions Serving the Seniors)
Limitation: No grants to individuals

SULZER FAMILY FOUNDATION
1940 West Irving Park Road
Chicago, IL 60613

Contact Person: John J. Hoellen, President
Geographic Giving Pattern: Primarily local - Ravenswood, Lakeview areas
of Chicago
Special Interest: Church support and religious organizations
Religious Preference: Protestant, Roman Catholic, Jewish
Assets: $1,700,122
Grant Range: $5,000 - $100

Indiana

HILLENBRAND (JOHN A.) FOUNDATION
Highway 46
Batesville, IN 47006
(812) 934-7000

Contact Person: William A. Hillenbrand, President
Geographic Giving Pattern: Primarily Batesville and Ripley County, IN
Special Interest: Church support
Religious Preference: Protestant, Roman Catholic
Assets: $3,434,793
Grant Range: $49,000 - $500
Limitation: Initial Approach: Typewritten Letter

IRWIN-SWEENEY-MILLER FOUNDATION
420 Third Street
Columbus, IN 47202
(812) 372-0251

Contact Person: John L. Lewis, Program Officer
Geographic Giving Pattern: Primarily local
Special Interest: Religious, the arts, social justice, education
Religious Preference: Protestant, Roman Catholic, Jewish
Assets: $3,052,346
Grant Range: $50,000 - $1,000 (Denominational)
Limitation: New funding is currently limited to organizations in
Columbus, IN area

LILLY ENDOWMENT, INC.
2801 North Meridian Street
P.O. Box 88068
Indianapolis, IN 46208
(317) 924-5471
Contact Person: Robert Lynn, Vice-President - Religion
Geographic Giving Pattern: National
Special Interest: Theological seminaries, Black church leadership, youth ministry
Religious Preference: Protestant, Roman Catholic, Jewish
Assets: $889,616,965
Grant Range: $200,000 - $10,000 (Religious Education/Religion)

Massachusetts

ALDEN (GEORGE I.) TRUST
370 Main Street, Suite 1250
Worcester, MA 01608
(617) 757-9243
Contact Person: Paris Fletcher, Chairman
Special Interest: Higher education, including theological seminaries
Assets: $51,141,000
Grant Range: $300,000 - $1,000
Limitation: No grants to individuals

JOHNSON (HOWARD) FOUNDATION, THE
One Howard Johnson Plaza
Dorchester, MA 02125
(617) 847-2000
Contact Person: Eugene J. Durgin, Secretary
Geographic Giving Pattern: National
Special Interest: Religious welfare, education, health and church support
Religious Preference: Roman Catholic, Protestant
Assets: $3,052,768
Grant Range: $25,000 - $1,000
Limitation: No gifts to individuals

SAWYER CHARITABLE FOUNDATION
209 Columbus Avenue, 5th Floor
Boston, MA 02116
(617) 267-2414

Contact Person: Carol S. Parks, Executive Director
Special Interest: Religious, educational, humanitarian
Religious Preference: Roman Catholic, Jewish
Assets: $2,949,475
Grant Range: $25,000 - $25

Michigan

FORD MOTOR COMPANY FUND
The American Road
Dearborn, MI
(313) 845-8711

Contact Person: Leo J. Brennan, Jr., Executive Director
Geographic Giving Pattern: Nationwide in areas where the company has plant locations, with special emphasis on Detroit and MI
Assets: $48,156,324
Grant Range: $200,000 - $1,000

KRESGE FOUNDATION, THE
3215 W. Big Beaver Road
P.O. Box 3151
Troy, MI 48084
(313) 643-9630

Contact Person: Alfred H. Taylor, Jr., President
Geographic Giving Pattern: National
Special Interest: Building projects
Religious Preference: Protestant, Roman Catholic, Jewish
Assets: $813,648,263
Grant Range: $3,000,000 - $25,000
Limitation: No grants to individuals or for endowment funds

MCGREGOR FUND
333 West Fort Building, Suite 1380
Detroit, MI 48226
(313) 963-3495

Contact Person: Jack L. Otto, Executive Director
Geographic Giving Pattern: Primarily Detroit metropolitan area and MI
Special Interest: Education, humanities and sciences
Religious Preference: Protestant, Roman Catholic, Jewish
Assets: $51,543,035
Grant Range: $200,000 - $2,000
Limitation: No grants to individuals

Minnesota

BREMER (OTTO) FOUNDATION
55 E. Fifth Street, Suite 700
St. Paul, MN 55101
(612) 227-8036
Contact Person: John Kustishack, Executive Director
Geographic Giving Pattern: MN, ND, WI and the city of St. Paul
Special Interest: Post-secondary education, human services, health,
religion, community affairs
Assets: $59,707,010
Grant Range: $11,000 - $1,000 (Religious)

RIVERS (MARGARET) FUND
C/o William D. Klapp
First National Bank Building
Stillwater, MN 55082
(612) 439-4411
Contact Person: William D. Klapp, President
Geographic Giving Pattern: Primarily local
Special Interest: Church support
Religious Preference: Protestant, Roman Catholic, Jewish
Assets: $9,648,703
Grant Range: $25,000 - $500

Missouri

GAYLORD (CATHERINE MANLEY) FOUNDATION, THE
314 N. Broadway, Room 1230
St. Louis, MO 63102
(314) 421-0181
Contact Person: Donald E. Fahey, Trustee
Geographic Giving Pattern: Primarily local
Special Interest: Church support, education, childwelfare and homes for
the aged
Religious Preference: Protestant, Roman Catholic, Jewish
Assets: $3,664,066
Grant Range: $25,000 - $1,000 (Religious)
Limitation: No grants to individuals

New York

ALTMAN FOUNDATION
361 Fifth Avenue
New York, NY 10016
(212) 679-7800

Contact Person: John S. Burke, President
Geographic Giving Pattern: New York state
Special Interest: To aid charitable and educational institutions with emphasis on religious associations
Religious Preference: Protestant, Roman Catholic, Jewish
Assets: $87,897,598
Grant Range: $100,000 - $1,000

BOOTH FERRIS FOUNDATION
30 Broad Street
New York, NY 10004
(212) 269-3850

Contact Person: Robert J. Murtagh, Trustee
Geographic Giving Pattern: National
Special Interest: Theological seminaries
Religious Preference: Protestant, Roman Catholic, Jewish
Assets: $81,681,833
Grant Range: $70,000 - $15,000 (Religion/Theological Education)

CLARK (FRANK E.) CHARITABLE TRUST
c/o Manufacturers Hanover Trust Company
600 Fifth Avenue
New York, NY 10020
(212) 957-1426

Contact Person: Helen M. Thome, Vice-President; (212) 957-1662
Geographic Giving Pattern: Primarily local
Special Interest: Charitable and religious purposes. Income is distributed to the parent body of major religious denominations for aid to needy churches
Assets: $2,560,489
Grant Range: $14,100 - $400
Limitation: Application deadline: October 31

COLT (JAMES J.) FOUNDATION, INC.
375 Park Avenue
New York, NY 10022
(212) 371-1110

Contact Person: Miss Lottie L. Jeffers, Secretary-Treasurer
Geographic Giving Pattern: Primarily local
Special Interest: Hospitals, welfare funds, church support
Religious Preference: Protestant, Roman Catholic, Jewish
Assets: $2,369,749
Grant Range: $35,000 - $50

CONSTANS-CULVER FOUNDATION
c/o Manufacturers Hanover Trust Company
600 Fifth Avenue
New York, NY 10020
(212) 957-1522
Contact Person: Robert Rosenthal, Vice-President; (212) 957-1500
Geographic Giving Pattern: Primarily local
Special Interest: Church support
Religious Preference: Protestant, Roman Catholic, Jewish
Assets: $3,397,749
Grant Range: $22,500 - $500

DULA (CALEB C. AND JULIA W.) EDUCATIONAL AND CHARITABLE
FOUNDATION, THE
c/o Manufacturers Hanover Trust Company
600 Fifth Avenue
New York, NY 10020
(212) 957-1222
Contact Person: Manufacturers Hanover Trust Co., Trustee
M.J.A. Smith, Administrative Officer
Geographic Giving Pattern: Primarily New York and St. Louis, MO
Special Interest: Church support
Religious Preference: Greek Orthodox, Episcopalian
Assets: $12,587,959
Grant Range: $100,000 - $500

EBSARY CHARITABLE FOUNDATION,THE
80 Rockwood Place
Rochester, NY 14610
(716) 224-0256
Contact Person: Frank W. Allen, President
Geographic Giving Pattern: Primarily local
Special Interest: Protestant and Roman Catholic church support, higher
education, welfare, youth agencies, cultural organizations
Assets: $918,429
Grant Range: $10,000 - $250 (Religious)

GOODMAN FAMILY FOUNDATION, THE
c/o Roy M. Goodman
1035 Fifth Avenue
New York, NY 10028
(212) 288-9067

Contact Person: Roy M. Goodman, President
Geographic Giving Pattern: Primarily local
Special Interest: Church and temple support, hospitals, and medical research
Religious Preference: Protestant, Roman Catholic, Jewish
Assets: $2,445,945
Grant Range: $11,000 - $100

HAGEDORN FUND, THE
c/o Manufacturers Hanover Trust Co.
600 Fifth Avenue
New York, NY 10020
(212) 957-1500

Contact Person: Robert Rosenthal, Asst. Vice-President
Geographic Giving Pattern: Primarily New York
Special Interest: Theological seminaries, church support, religious associations
Religious Preference: Protestant, Roman Catholic, Jewish
Assets: $3,107,621
Grant Range: $22,500 - $500

HEARST FOUNDATION, INC., THE
888 Seventh Avenue, 27th Floor
New York, NY 10106
(212) 586-5404

Contact Person: Robert M. Freshe, Jr., Executive Director for programs headquartered east of the Mississippi River
Geographic Giving Pattern: Within the United States and possessions
Special Interest: Poverty level and minority groups, education at all levels, health and medical research, cultural and religious programs
Religious Preference: Protestant, Roman Catholic, Jewish
Assets: $65,470,270
Grant Range: $15,000 - $5,000 (Denominational Giving)
Limitation: No grants to individuals

KRESEVICH FOUNDATION, INC., THE
184 W. 237 Street
Bronx, NY 10463

Contact Person: Felice Zambetti, President
Special Interest: Roman Catholic religious associations, church support. Some support for Jewish programs
Assets: $818,395
Grant Range: $40,000 - $10

LUCE (HENRY) FOUNDATION, INC., THE
111 W. 50th Street
New York, NY 10020
(212) 489-7700

Contact Person: Robert E. Armstrong, Executive Director
Geographic Giving Pattern: National, international
Special Interest: Theology
Religious Preference: Protestant, Roman Catholic, Jewish
Assets: $205,053,017
Grant Range: $500,000 - $5,000
Limitation: International activities confined to East and Southeast Asia

MCCANN FOUNDATION, THE
(JAMES J. MCCANN CHARITABLE TRUST & MCCANN
FOUNDATION, INC.)
35 Market Street
Poughkeepsie, NY 12601
(914) 452-3085

Contact Person: John J. Gartland, Jr., Trustee
Geographic Giving Pattern: Primarily Dutchess County, New York
Special Interest: Education and research, arts, community service, health and medicine, church and religious associations
Religious Preference: Protestant, Roman Catholic, Jewish
Assets: $20,105,478
Grant Range: $22,205 - $1,900 (Denominational Giving)
Limitation: No grants to individuals or endowment funds

MICHEL (BARBARA AND CLIFFORD) FOUNDATION, INC.
80 Pine Street
New York, NY 10005
(212) 344-3091

Contact Person: James E. Alexander, Treasurer
Geographic Giving Pattern: Primarily local
Special Interest: Church support, education, hospitals
Religious Preference: Protestant, Roman Catholic, Jewish
Assets: $691,500
Grant Range: $25,000 - $1,000

MONTEREY FUND, INC.
c/o Bear, Stearns & Company
5 Hanover Square
New York, NY 10004

Contact Person: Carl Holstrom, President
Geographic Giving Pattern: Primarily local
Special Interest: Educational institutions, welfare funds, hospitals, churches and synagogues
Religious Preference: Jewish, Roman Catholic, Protestant
Assets: $2,972,525
Grant Range: $175,250 - $100

ROCKEFELLER BROTHERS FUND
1290 Avenue of the Americas
New York, NY 10104
(212) 397-4800

Contact Person: Benjamin R. Shute, Jr., Secretary
Geographic Giving Pattern: National, international
Religious Preference: Protestant, Roman Catholic
Assets: $172,859,783
Grant Range: $15,000,000 - $2,000

ROCKEFELLER FOUNDATION, THE
1133 Avenue of the Americas
New York, NY 10036
(212) 869-8500

Contact Person: Simon P. Gourdine, Secretary
Geographic Giving Pattern: National, international
Religious Preference: Protestant, Roman Catholic, Jewish
Assets: $1,101,856,013
Grant Range: $987,500 - $1,025

North Carolina

BLUMENTHAL FOUNDATION, THE
P.O. Box 34689
Charlotte, NC 28234
(704) 377-6555

Contact Person: Herman Blumenthal, Chairman
Geographic Giving Pattern: Primarily in North Carolina
Special Interest: Conferences to promote understanding among religions. Also supports religious, educational, and welfare organizations
Religious Preference: Protestant, Roman Catholic, Jewish

Assets: $16,206,452
Grant Range: $145,350 - $15

RIXSON (OSCAR C.) FOUNDATION, INC.
535 Glendale Drive
Statesville, NC 28677
(704) 837-1550

Contact Person: Walter J. Munro, Jr., President
Special Interest: Needy active and retired religious workers. Also religious charitable organizations
Religious Preference: Protestant, Roman Catholic

Assets: $1,500,739
Grant Range: $10,000 - $100

Ohio

ANDERSON FOUNDATION
P.O. Box 119
Maumee, OH 43537
(419) 893-5050

Contact Person: Tammy Samahaj, Secretary to the Chairman
Geographic Giving Pattern: Primarily Toledo, Ohio
Special Interest: Education, religious organizations, churches, community funds
Religious Preference: Protestant, Roman Catholic, Jewish

Assets: $4,422,743
Grant Range: $31,500 - $375 (Denominational Giving)
Limitation: No grants to individuals

VAN HUFFEL (I.J.) FOUNDATION, THE
Bank One of Eastern Ohio
106 Market Street
Warren, OH 44481
(216) 841-7000

Contact Person: Bank One of Eastern Ohio, National Trustee
Geographic Giving Pattern: National
Special Interest: Religious, educational, charitable
Religious Preference: Protestant, Roman Catholic

Assets: $1,402,996
Grant Range: $11,000 - $750 (Religious)

Oregon

COLLINS FOUNDATION
909 Terminal Sales Building
Portland, OR 97205
(503) 227-1219

Contact Person: William C. Pine, Executive Vice-President
Geographic Giving Pattern: Oregon
Special Interest: Education - higher and secondary, particularly science education; church support, youth and health agencies, social welfare
Religious Preference: Protestant, Roman Catholic

Assets: $45,349,237
Grant Range: $15,000 - $1,200 (Religious)
Limitation: No grants to individuals

Pennsylvania

CONNELLY FOUNDATION
9300Ashton Road
Philadelphia, PA 19136
(215) 698-5203

Contact Person: John F. Connelly, President
Geographic Giving Pattern: Primarily Philadelphia
Special Interest: Universities, colleges, schools, churches and hospitals
Religious Preference: Protestant, Roman Catholic, Jewish

Assets: $2,236,978
Grant Range: $17,000 - $1,000
Limitation: Contributions to pre-selected organizations only

Texas

ABELL-HANGER FOUNDATION
Firs National Bank Building, Room 615
Midland, TX 79701
(915) 684-6655
Mailing address: P.O. Box 430
Midland, TX 79702

Contact Person: David L. Smith, Manager
Geographic Giving Pattern: Limited to Texas
Assets: $49,224,386
Grant Range: $250,000 - $5,000
Limitation: No grants to individuals. No loans

BROWN FOUNDATION, INC., THE
2118 Welch Avenue
P.O. Box 13646
Houston, TX 77219
(713) 523-6867

Contact Person: Katherine B. Dobelman, Executive Director
Geographic Giving Pattern: Primarily in Texas with emphasis on Houston
Assets: $241,534,233
Grant Range: $500,000 - $5,000
Limitation: No grants to individuals. No loans

FARISH (WILLIAM STAMPS) FUND, THE
1100 Louisiana, Suite 4500
Houston, TX 77002
(713) 757-7313

Contact Person: W.S. Farish, III, President
Geographic Giving Pattern: Primarily local
Special Interest: Theological seminaries, Episcopal church support
Religious Preference: Protestant, Roman Catholic

Assets: $52,654,336
Grant Range: $39,000 - $3,000 (Denominational Giving)
Limitation: No grants to individuals

HOUSTON ENDOWMENT, INC.
P.O. Box 52338
Houston, TX 77052
(713) 223-4043

Contact Person: Marshall F. Wells, Grants Coordinator
Geographic Giving Pattern: Primarily in Texas. No grants outside the continental U.S.

Assets: $303,416,058
Grant Range: $1,000,000 - $5,000
Limitation: No grants to individuals. No loans

O'CONNOR (KATHRYN) FOUNDATION, THE
400 Victoria Bank & Trust Building
Victoria, TX 77901
(512) 578-6271

Contact Person: Dennis O'Connor, President
Geographic Giving Pattern: Primarily local
Special Interest: Advancement of religion, education and relief of poverty
Religious Preference: Protestant, Roman Catholic

Assets: $5,128,114
Grant Range: $104,324 - $1,000
Limitation: No grants to individuals

SAN ANTONIO AREA FOUNDATION
808 Travis Building
405 North St. Mary's
San Antonio, TX 78205
(512) 225-2243

Contact Person: Katherine Netting Folbre, Executive Director
Geographic Giving Pattern: Limited to San Antonio, except when specified otherwise by donor
Religious Preference: All denominations
Assets: $7,799,838
Grant Range: $24,000 - $5,000

Virginia

WASHINGTON FORREST FOUNDATION
2300 Ninth Street, South
Arlington, VA 22204
(703) 920-2200

Contact Person: Lindsey Peete
Geographic Giving Pattern: Northern Virginia
Special Interest: Religion, education, arts and humanities, health, science, welfare
Religious Preference: Protestant, Roman Catholic
Assets: $5,117,419
Grant Range: $18,000 - $500

Wisconsin

CUDAHY (PATRICK AND ANNA M.) FUND
P.O. Box 11978
Milwaukee, WI 53211
(414) 962-6820

Contact Person: Richard W. Yeo, Administrator
Geographic Giving Pattern: Primarily local
Religious Preference: Protestant, Roman Catholic, Jewish
Assets: $14,662,792
Grant Range: $10,000 - $1,000 (Denominational Giving)
Limitation: No grants to individuals or for endowment funds

VILTER FOUNDATION, INC.
2217 South First Street
Milwaukee, WI 53207
(414) 744-0111

Contact Person: A.A. Silverman, President
Geographic Giving Pattern: Primarily local
Special Interest: Churches, education - higher and secondary, religious welfare funds
Religious Preference: Protestant, Roman Catholic, Jewish
Assets: $2,873,333
Grant Range: $15,000 - $100

OTHER FOUNDATIONS

Alabama

MALBIS MEMORIAL FOUNDATION
c/o Antigone Papageorge
P.O. Box 218
Daphne, AL 36526
(205) 626-3050

Contact Person: C.D. Papadeas, President
Geographic Giving Pattern: Primarily in the S.E., particularly in AL
Special Interest: Primarily religious; Greek Orthodox
Assets: $1,927,520
Grant Range: $6,850 - $100

California

PEERY (RICHARD T.) FOUNDATION
2560 Mission College Blvd., Suite 101
Santas Clara, CA 95000
(408) 980-0130

Contact Person: Richard T. Peery
Geographic Giving Pattern: International
Special Interest: Mormon Church
Assets: $3,041,748
Grant Range: $127,693 - $300

PHILIBOSIAN (STEPHEN) FOUNDATION
46930 W. Eldorado Drive
Indian Wells, CA 92260
(619) 568-3920

Contact Person: Joyce Stein, Trustee
Geographic Giving Pattern: International
Special Interest: Missionary, educational and social programs for the
Armenian-American church including aid for Armenian schools in the
Middle East
Assets: $5,535,695
Grant Range: $229,920 - $50
Limitation: No grants to individuals

Kansas

SCHOWALTER FOUNDATION, INC., THE
716 Main Street
Newton, KS 67114
(316) 283-3720
Contact Person: William L. Friesen, President
Geographic Giving Pattern: Primarily Midwest, some international
Special Interest: Retired ministers and missionaries, theological seminaries and church-related schools
Religious Preference: Mennonite
Assets: $4,576,147
Grant Range: $25,000 - $2,000

Louisiana

HELIS FOUNDATION, THE
912 Whitney Building
New Orleans, LA 70130
(504) 523-1831
Contact Person: A.E. Armbruster, Vice-President
Geographic Giving Pattern: Primarily local
Special Interest: Support for church and religious organizations, higher education
Religious Preference: Greek Orthodox
Assets: $7,579,569
Grant Range: $60,000 - $250

Massachusetts

DEMOULAS FOUNDATION
875 East Street
Tewksbury, MA 01876
(6127) 851-7381
Contact Person: Telemachus A. Demoulas
Geographic Giving Pattern: Primarily local
Special Interest: Greek Orthodox church support, higher and secondary education
Assets: $14,656,915
Grant Range: $469,819 for 294 grants

Michigan

MANOOGIAN (ALEX AND MARIA) FOUNDATION
3001 W. Big Beaver, Suite 520
Troy, MI 48084

Contact Person: Alex Manoogian, President
Geographic Giving Pattern: General
Special Interest: Armenian welfare funds, religious organizations, churches, education and cultural programs
Assets: $25,948,904
Grant Range: $117,120 - $100 (Armenian Religious Giving)

MARDIGIAN FOUNDATION
1525 Tottenham
Birmingham, MI 48009
(313) 589-3804

Contact Person: Edward Mardigian, Sr., President
Geographic Giving Pattern: National
Special Interest: Armenian church and cultural support, religious associations and welfare funds
Assets: $3,345,446
Grant Range: $4,600 - $10 (Religious)

Appendix A

The Foundation Center has a nationwide network of reference collections for free public use which fall within four basic categories. The reference libraries operated by the Center offer the widest variety of user services and the most comprehensive collections of foundation materials, including all Center publications; books, services and periodicals on philanthropy; and foundation annual reports, newsletters and press clippings. The New York and Washington, D.C. libraries contain the IRS returns for all currently active private foundations in the U.S. The Cleveland and San Francisco field offices contain IRS records for those foundations in the midwestern and western states, respectively.

Cooperating collections contain IRS records for those foundations within their own state, and a complete collection of Foundation Center publications. Local affiliate collections (*) provide a core collection of Center publications for free public use.

Some reference collections (•) are operated by foundations or area associations of foundations. They are often able to offer special materials or provide extra services, such as seminars or orientations for users, because of their close relationship to the local philanthropic community. All other collections are operated by cooperating libraries or other nonprofit agencies. Many are located within public institutions and all are open to the public during a regular schedule of hours.

Please telephone individual libraries for more information about their holdings or hours. To check on new locations call toll-free 800-424-9836 for current information.

Where to Go for Information on Foundation Funding

REFERENCE COLLECTIONS OPERATED BY THE FOUNDATION CENTER

The Foundation Center
79 Fifth Avenue
NEW YORK, New York 10003
212-620-4230

The Foundation Center
1001 Connecticut Avenue, NW
WASHINGTON, D.C. 20036
202-331-1400

The Foundation Center
Kent H. Smith Library
1442 Hanna Building
1422 Euclid Avenue
CLEVELAND, Ohio 44115
216-861-1933

The Foundation Center
312 Sutter Street
SAN FRANCISCO, California 94108
415-397-0902

COOPERATING COLLECTIONS

Alabama

Birmingham Public Library •
2020 Park Place
Birmingham 35203
205-226-3600

Huntsville—Madison County Public Library
108 Fountain Circle
P.O. Box 443
Huntsville 35804
205-536-0021

Auburn University at Montgomery Library
Montgomery 36193-0401
205-271-9649

Alaska

University of Alaska, Anchorage Library •
3211 Providence Drive
Anchorage 99504
907-786-1848

Arizona

Phoenix Public Library •
Business and Sciences Department
12 East McDowell Road
Phoenix 85004
602-262-4782

Tucson Public Library •
Main Library
200 South Sixth Avenue
Tucson 85701
607-791-4393

Arkansas

Westark Community College Library •
Grand Avenue at Waldron Road
Fort Smith 72913
501-785-4241

Little Rock Public Library •
Reference Department
700 Louisiana Street
Little Rock 72201
501-370-5950

California

Inyo County Library—Bishop Branch
210 Academy Street
Bishop 93514
619-872-8091

California Community Foundation •
Funding Information Center
3580 Wilshire Boulevard, Suite 1660
Los Angeles 90010
213-413-4042

Community Foundation for Monterey County •
420 Pacific Street
Monterey 93940
408-375-9712

California Community Foundation
4050 Metropolitan Drive #300
Orange 92668
714-937-9077

Riverside Public Library *
3581 7th Street
Riverside 92501
714-787-7201

California State Library *
Reference Services, Room 309
914 Capitol Mall
Sacramento 95814
916-322-4570

San Diego Community Foundation
625 Broadway, Suite 1015
San Diego 92101
619-239-8815

Orange County Community Development Council *
1440 East First Street, 4th floor
Santa Ana 92701
714-547-6801

Penisula Community Foundation
1204 Burlingame Avenue
Burlingame 94011-0627
415-342-2505

Santa Barbara Public Library •
Reference Section
40 East Anapamu
P.O. Box 1019
Santa Barbara 93102
805-962-7653

Santa Monica Public Library
1343 Sixth Street
Santa Monica 90401-1603
213-458-8603

Tuolomne County Library
465 S. Washington Street
Sonora 95370
209-533-5707

North Coast Opportunities, Inc. *
101 West Church Street
Ukiah 95482
707-462-1954

Colorado

Pikes Peak Library District *
20 North Cascade Avenue
Colorado Springs 80901
303-473-2080

Denver Public Library •
Sociology Division
1357 Broadway
Denver 80203
303-571-2190

Connecticut

Danbury Public Library
155 Deer Hill Avenue
Danbury 06810
203-797-4505

Hartford Public Library •
Reference Department
500 Main Street
Hartford 06103
203-525-9121

D.A.T.A.
800 Asylum Avenue
Hartford 06105
203-278-2477

D.A.T.A. *
25 Science Park, Suite 502
New Haven 06513
203-786-5225

Delaware

Hugh Morris Library •
University of Delaware
Newark 19717-5267
302-451-2965

Florida

Volusia County Public Library
City Island
Daytona Beach 32014
904-252-8374

Jacksonville Public Library *
Business, Science, and Industry Department
122 North Ocean Street
Jacksonville 32202
904-633-3926

Miami-Dade Public Library •
Florida Collection
One Biscayne Boulevard
Miami 33132
305-579-5001

Orlando Public Library •
10 North Rosalind
Orlando 32801
305-425-4694

University of W. Florida •
John C. Pace Library
Pensacola 32514
904-474-2412

Selby Public Library •
1001 Boulevard of the Arts
Sarasota 33577
813-366-7303

Leon County Public Library •
Community Funding Resources Center
1940 North Monroe Street
Tallahassee 32303
904-478-2665

Palm Beach County Community Foundation
324 Datura Street, Suite 311
West Palm Beach 33401
305-659-6800

Georgia

Atlanta-Fulton Public Library •
Ivan Allen Department
1 Margaret Mitchell Square
Atlanta 30303
404-688-4636

Hawaii

Thomas Hale Hamilton Library •
General Reference
University of Hawaii
2550 The Mall
Honolulu 96822
808-948-7214

Community Research Center * •
The Hawaiian Foundation
Financial Plaza of the Pacific
111 South King Street
Honolulu 96813
808-525-8548

Idaho

Caldwell Public Library •
1010 Dearborn Street
Caldwell 83605
208-459-3242

Illinois

Belleville Public Library *
121 E. Washington Steet
Belleville 62220
618-234-0441

Donors Forum of Chicago •
208 South LaSalle Street
Chicago 60604
312-726-4882

DuPage Township *
300 Briarcliff Road
Bolingbrook 60439
312-759-1317

Evanston Public Library •
1703 Orrington Avenue
Evanston 60201
312-866-0305

Sangamon State University Library •
Shepherd Road
Springfield 62708
217-786-6633

Indiana

Allen County Public Library *
900 Webster Street
Fort Wayne 46802
219-424-7241

Indiana University Northwest Library *
3400 Broadway
Gary 46408
219-980-6580

Indianapolis-Marion County Public Library •
40 East St. Clair Street
Indianapolis 46204
317-269-1733

Iowa

Public Library of Des Moines
100 Locust Street
Des Moines 50308
515-283-4259

Kansas

Topeka Public Library •
Adult Services Department
1515 West Tenth Street
Topeka 66604
913-233-2040

Wichita Public Library •
223 South Main
Wichita 67202
316-262-0611

Kentucky

Western Kentucky University •
Division of Library Services
Helm-Cravens Library
Bowling Green 42101
502-745-3951

Louisville Free Public Library •
Fourth and York Streets
Louisville 40203
503-223-7201

Louisiana

East Baton Rouge Parish Library •
Centroplex Library
120 St. Louis Street
Baton Rouge 70821
504-389-4960

New Orleans Public Library •
Business and Science Division
219 Loyola Avenue
New Orleans 70140
504-596-2583

Shreve Memorial Library •
424 Texas Street
Shreveport 71101
318-226-5894

Maine

University of Southern Maine •
Center for Research and Advanced Study
246 Deering Avenue
Portland 04102
207-780-4411

Maryland

Enoch Pratt Free Library •
Social Science and History Department
400 Cathedral Street
Baltimore 21201
301-396-5320

Massachusetts

Associated Grantmakers of Massachusetts •
294 Washington Street, Suite 501
Boston 02108
617-426-2608

Boston Public Library •
Copley Square
Boston 02117
617-536-5400

Walpole Public Library •
Common Street
Walpole 02018
617-668-5497, ext. 340

Western Massachusetts Funding Resource Center *
Campaign for Human Development
Chancery Annex
73 Chestnut Street
Springfield 01103
413-732-3175, ext. 67

Grants Resource Center •
Worcester Public Library
Salem Square
Worcester 01608
617-799-1655

Michigan

Alpena County Library *
211 North First Avenue
Alpena 49707
517-356-6188

University of Michigan-Ann Arbor
Reference Department
209 Hatcher Graduate Library
Ann Arbor 48109-1205
313-764-1149

Henry Ford Centennial Library •
16301 Michigan Avenue
Dearborn 48126
313-943-2337

Purdy Library •
Wayne State University
Detroit 48202
313-577-4040

Michigan State University Libraries •
Reference Library
East Lansing 48824
517-353-9184

Farmington Community Library •
32737 West 12 Mile Road
Farmington Hills 48018
313-553-0300

University of Michigan-Flint Library •
Reference Department
Flint 48503
313-762-3408

Grand Rapids Public Library
Sociology and Education Department
Library Plaza
Grand Rapids 49502
616-456-4411

Michigan Technological University Library
Highway U.S. 41
Houghton 49931
906-487-2507

Minnesota

Duluth Public Library •
520 Superior Street
Duluth 55802
218-723-3802

Southwest State University Library •
Marshall 56258
507-537-7278

Minneapolis Public Library •
Sociology Department
300 Nicollet Mall
Minneapolis 55401
612-372-6555

Rochester Public Library
Broadway and First Street, S.E.
Rochester 55901
507-285-8002

St. Paul Public Library *
90 West Fourth Street
Saint Paul 55102
612-292-6311

Mississippi

Jackson Metropolitan Library
301 North State Street
Jackson 39201
601-944-1120

Missouri

Clearinghouse for Midcontinent Foundations •
University of Missouri, Kansas City
Law School, Suite 1-300
52nd Street and Oak
Kansas City 64113
816-276-1176

Kansas City Public Library •
311 East 12th Street
Kansas City 64106
816-221-2685

Metropolitan Association for Philanthropy, Inc. •
5585 Pershing Avenue, Suite 150
St. Louis 63112
314-361-3900

Springfield-Greene County Library •
397 East Central Street
Springfield 65801
417-866-4636

Montana

Eastern Montana College Library •
Reference Department
1500 N. 30th Street
Billings 59101-0298
406-657-2262

Montana State Library •
Reference Department
1515 E. 6th Avenue
Helena 59620
406-444-3004

Nebraska

University of Nebraska, Lincoln
106 Love Library
Lincoln 68588-0410
402-472-2526

W. Dale Clark Library •
Social Sciences Department
215 South 15th Street
Omaha 68102
402-444-4822

Nevada

Las Vegas-Clark County Library District •
1401 East Flamingo Road
Las Vegas 89109
702-733-7810

Washoe County Library •
301 South Center Street
Reno 89505
702-785-4190

New Hampshire

The New Hampshire Charitable Fund •
One South Street
Concord 03301
603-225-6641

Littleton Public Library •
109 Main Street
Littleton 03561
603-444-5741

New Jersey

Cumberland County Library
800 E. Commerce Street
Bridgeton 08302
609-455-0080

The Support Center *
17 Academy Street, Suite 1101
Newark 07102
201-643-5774

County College of Morris
Masten Learning Resource Center
Route 10 and Center Grove Road
Randolph 07869
201-361-5000, ext. 470

New Jersey State Library
Government Reference Unit
185 West State Street
P.O. Box 1898
Trenton 08625
609-292-6220

New Mexico

Albuquerque Community Foundation • *
6400 Uptown Boulevard, N.E., Suite 500-W
Albuquerque 87110
505-883-6240

New Mexico State Library •
325 Don Gaspar Street
Santa Fe 87503
505-827-3824

New York

New York State Library •
Cultural Education Center
Humanities Section
Empire State Plaza
Albany 12230
518-474-7645

Bronx Reference Center
New York Public Library
2556 Bainbridge Avenue
Bronx 10458
212-220-6575

Brooklyn in Touch
101 Willoughby Street, Room 1508
Brooklyn 11201
718-237-9300

Buffalo and Erie County Public Library •
Lafayette Square
Buffalo 14203
716-856-7525

Huntington Public Library
338 Main Street
Huntington 11743
516-427-5165

Levittown Public Library •
Reference Department
One Bluegrass Lane
Levittown 11756
516-731-5728

SUNY/College at Old Westbury Library
223 Store Hill Road
Old Westbury 11568
516-876-3201

Plattsburgh Public Library •
Reference Department
15 Oak Street
Plattsburgh 12901
518-563-0921

Adriance Memorial Library
93 Market Street
Poughkeepsie 12601
914-485-4790

Queens Borough Public Library
89-11 Merrick Boulevard
Jamaica 11432
718-990-0700

Rochester Public Library •
Business and Social Sciences Division
115 South Avenue
Rochester 14604
716-428-7328

Staten Island Council on the Arts
One Edgewater Plaza, Room 311
Staten Island 10305
718-447-4485

Onondaga County Public Library •
335 Montgomery Street
Syracuse 13202
315-473-4491

White Plains Public Library *
100 Martine Avenue
White Plains 10601
914-682-4488

North Carolina

The Duke Endowment •
200 S. Tryon Street, Suite 1100
Charlotte 28202
704-376-0291

Durham County Library
300 N. Roxoboro Street
Durham 27701
919-683-2626

North Carolina State Library •
109 East Jones Street
Raleigh 27611
919-733-3270

The Winston-Salem Foundation •
229 First Union National Bank Building
Winston-Salem 27101
919-725-2382

North Dakota

Western Dakota Grants Resource Center *
Bismarck Junior College Library
Bismarck 58501
701-224-5450

The Library, North Dakota State University •
Fargo 58105
701-237-8876

Ohio

Public Library of Cincinnati and Hamilton County •
Education Department
800 Vine Street
Cincinnati 45202
513-369-6940

Public Library of Columbus and Franklin County •
28 S. Hamilton Road
Columbus 43213-2097
614-222-7180

Dayton and Montgomery County Public Library
Social Sciences Department
213 E. Third Street
Dayton 45402
513-224-1651

Lima-Allen County Regional Planning Commission
212 Elizabeth Street
Lima 45801
419-228-1836

Toledo-Lucas County Public Library •
Social Science Department
325 Michigan Street
Toledo 43624
419-255-7055, ext. 221

Ohio University-Zanesville
Community Education and Development
1425 Newark Road
Zanesville 43701
614-453-0762

Oklahoma

Oklahoma City University Library •
NW 23rd at North Blackwelder
Oklahoma City 73106
405-521-5072

The Support Center •
525 NW Thirteenth Street
Oklahoma City 73103
405-236-8133

Tulsa City-County Library System •
400 Civic Center
Tulsa 74103
918-592-7944

Oregon

Library Association of Portland •
Government Documents Room
801 S.W. Tenth Avenue
Portland 97205
503-223-7201

Oregon State Library
State Library Building
Salem 97310
503-378-4243

Pennsylvania

North Hampton County Area Community College *
Learning Resources Center
3835 Green Pond Road
Bethlehem 18017
215-865-5358

Erie County Public Library •
3 South Perry Square
Erie 16501
814-452-2333, ext. 54

Dauphin County Library System •
Central Library
101 Walnut Street
Harrisburg 17101
717-234-4961

Lancaster County Public Library *
125 North Duke Street
Lancaster 17602
717-394-2651

The Free Library of Philadelphia •
Logan Square
Philadelphia 19103
215-686-5423

Hillman Library •
University of Pittsburgh
Pittsburgh 15260
412-624-4423

Economic Development Council of
    Northeastern Pennsylvania •
1151 Oak Street
Pittston 18640
717-655-5581

James V. Brown Library
12 E. Fourth Street
Williamsport 17701
717-326-0536

Rhode Island

Providence Public Library •
Reference Department
150 Empire Street
Providence 02903
401-521-7722

South Carolina

Charleston County Public Library •
404 King Street
Charleston 29403
803-723-1645

South Carolina State Library •
Reader Services Department
1500 Senate Street
Columbia 29201
803-758-3138

South Dakota

South Dakota State Library •
State Library Building
800 N. Illinois Street
Pierre 57501
605-773-3131

Sioux Falls Area Foundation
404 Boyce Greeley Building
321 South Phillips Avenue
Sioux Falls 57102-0781
605-336-7055

Tennessee

Knoxville-Knox County Public Library •
500 West Church Avenue
Knoxville 37902
615-523-0781

Memphis-Shelby County Public Library
1850 Peabody Avenue
Memphis 38104
901-725-8876

Public Library of Nashville and Davidson County •
8th Avenue, North and Union Street
Nashville 37203
615-244-4700

Texas

Amarillo Area Foundation
1000 Polk
P.O. Box 25569
Amarillo 79105-569
806-376-4521

The Hogg Foundation for Mental Health •
The University of Texas
Austin 78712
512-471-5041

Corpus Christi State University Library
6300 Ocean Drive
Corpus Christi 78412
512-991-6810

El Paso Community Foundation •
El Paso National Bank Building, Suite 1616
El Paso 79901
915-533-4020

Funding Information Center •
Texas Christian University Library
Ft. Worth 76129
817-921-7664

Houston Public Library •
Bibliography and Information Center
500 McKinney Avenue
Houston 77002
713-224-5441, ext. 265

Funding Information Library •
507 Brooklyn
San Antonio 78215
512-227-4333

Dallas Public Library
Grants Information Service
1515 Young Street
Dallas 75201
214-749-4100

Pan American University
Learning Resource Center
1201 W. University Drive
Edinburg 78539
512-381-3304

Utah

Salt Lake City Public Library •
Business and Science Department
209 East Fifth South
Salt Lake City 84111
801-363-5733

Vermont

State of Vermont Department of Libraries •
References Services Unit
111 State Street
Montpellier 05602
802-828-3261

Virginia

Grants Resources Library •
Hampton City Hall
22 Lincoln Street, 9th floor
Hampton 23669
804-727-6496

Richmond Public Library •
Business, Science, and Technology Department
101 East Franklin Street
Richmond 23219
804-780-8223

Washington

Seattle Public Library •
1000 Fourth Avenue
Seattle 98104
206-625-4881

Spokane Public Library •
Funding Information Center
West 906 Main Avenue
Spokane 99201
509-838-3361

West Virginia

Kanawha County Public Library •
123 Capitol Street
Charleston 25301
304-343-4646

Wisconsin

Marquette University Memorial Library •
1415 West Wisconsin Avenue
Milwaukee 53233
414-224-1515

University of Wisconsin-Madison
Memorial Library
728 State Street
Madison 53706
608-262-3647

Society for Nonprofit Organizations
6314 Odana Road, Suite One
Madison 53719
608-274-9777

Wyoming

Laramie County Community College Library •
1400 East College Drive
Cheyenne 82007
307-634-5853

Canada

Canadian Centre for Philanthropy •
3080 Yonge Street, Suite 4080
Toronto, Ontario M4N 3N1
416-484-4118

England

Charities Aid Foundation *
14 Bloomsbury Square
London WC1A 2LP
01-430-1798

Marianna Islands

Northern Marianas College
P.O. Box 1250 CK
Saipan, GM 96950

Mexico

Biblioteca Benjamin Franklin
Londres 16
Mexico City 6, D.F.
525-591-0244

Puerto Rico

Universidad del Sagrado Corazon
M.M.T. Guevarra Library
Correo Galle Loiza
Santurce 00914
809-728-1515, ext. 274

Virgin Islands

College of the Virgin Islands Library
Saint Thomas
U.S. Virgin Islands 00801
809-774-9200, ext. 487

Appendix B

DIRECTORIES OF
STATE AND LOCAL GRANTMAKERS

A Bibliography Compiled by Lydia T. Motyka, Librarian

Alabama (184 foundations), *Alabama Foundation Directory.* Compiled by the Reference Department, Birmingham Public Library. 56 p. Based primarily on 1982 and 1983 990-PF returns filed with the IRS. Main section arranged alphabetically by foundation; entries include areas of interest and officers; no sample grants. Indexes of geographic areas and major areas of interest. Available from Reference Department, Birmingham Public Library, 2020 Park Place, Birmingham, Alabama 35203. $5.00 prepaid.

Alabama (212 foundations). *Foundation Profiles of the Southeast: Alabama, Arkansas, Louisiana, Mississippi.* Compiled by James H. Taylor and John L. Wilson. 1983. vi, 119 p. Based on 1978 and 1979 990-PF and 990-AR returns filed with the IRS. Main section arranged by state and alphabetically by foundation name; entries include principal officer, assets, total grants and sample grants. No indexes. Available from James H. Taylor Associates, Inc., 804 Main Street, Williamsburg, Kentucky 40769. $39.95 prepaid.

Arkansas (148 foundations). See **Alabama.**

Arkansas (97 + grantmakers). *Guide to Arkansas Funding Sources.* Compiled by Jerry Cronin and Cheryl Waller. 1983. 103 p. Based on 1980 and 1981 990-PF returns filed with the IRS. Main section arranged alphabetically under three categories: Arkansas foundations, foundations from neighboring states that make grants in Arkansas, and religious funding sources. Entries include assets, revenues and expenses, list of officers and trustees and sample grants. Appendix of smaller Arkansas foundations. Available from Independent Community Consultants, P.O. Box 1673, West Memphis, Arkansas 72301. $12.00 plus $1.50 postage and handling.

California (approximately 600 foundations). *Guide to California Foundations.* 5th edition. Prepared by Shelley Barclay. 1983. 512 p. Based primarily on 1982 990-PF returns filed with the IRS or records in the California Attorney General's Office; some additional data supplied by foundations completing questionnaires. Main section arranged alphabetically by foundation; entries include statement of purpose, sample grants and officers. Also section on applying for grants. Indexes of all foundations by name and county location; index of primary interest only for those foundations completing questionnaire. Available from Northern California Grantmakers, 334 Kearny Street, San Francisco, California 94108. $15.00 plus $2.00 tax and postage, prepaid.

California (620 corporations). *National Directory of Corporate Charity: California Edition.* Compiled by Sam Sternberg. 1981. x, 450+ p. Based on annual reports, questionnaires, reference directories, grants lists, corporate donors lists of nonprofit organizations, and news releases. Main section arranged alphabetically by corporation; entries include categories of giving, giving policies, geographic preference, and contact person; no sample grants. Also sections describing corporate giving patterns, nonprofit strategy and corporate giving, how to conduct a corporate solicitation campaign, and a bibliography. Indexes of operating locations of corporations, support categories, and companies and their California subsidiaries. Available from Regional Young Adult Project, 330 Ellis Street, Room 506, San Francisco, California 94102. $14.95 plus $2.00 shipping and sales tax for California residents.

California. (73 foundations). *San Diego County Foundation Directory 1980.* Compiled by the Community Congress of San Diego, Inc. 1980. 72 p. Based on 1977 through 1979 CT-2 forms with the California Attorney General's Office. Main section arranged alphabetically by foundation; entries include statement of purpose and contact person; no sample grants. Index of foundation names. Appendixes of San Diego County foundation grants, officers and trustees. Not available for purchase. May be used at the Community Congress of San Diego, 1172 Morena Boulevard, San Diego, California 92110, or the Foundation Center collection at the San Diego Community Foundation, 625 Broadway, Suite 1105, San Diego, California 92101.

California (45 Bay Area foundations). *Small Change from Big Bucks: A Report and Recommendations on Bay Area Foundations and Social Change.* Edited by Herb Allen and Sam Sternberg. 1979. 226 p. Based primarily on 1976 990-AR returns filed with the IRS, CT-2 forms filed with California, annual reports, and interviews with foundations. Main section arranged alphabetically by foundation; entries include statement of purpose and contact person; no sample grants. Also sections on the Bay Area Committee for Responsive Philanthropy, foundations and social change, the study methodology, the committee's findings, and the committee's recommendations. No indexes. Appendixes of Bay Area resources for technical assistance, bibliography, nonprofit organizations in law and fact, and glossary. Available from Regional Young Adult Project, 330 Ellis Street, Room 506, San Francisco, California 94102. Make check payable to: Regional Young Adult Project. $3.00 plus $1.50 postage.

California (525 foundations). *Where the Money's At, How to Reach Over 500 California Grant-Making Foundations.* Edited by Patricia Blair Tobey with Irving R. Warner as contributing editor. 1978. 536 p. Based on 1975 through 1977 (mainly 1976) California CT-2 forms in the California Registry of Charitable Trusts Office. Main section arranged alphabetically by foundation; entries include statement of purpose, sample grants and officers. Indexes of foundation names, foundation names within either Northern of Southern California, counties, and foundation personnel. Available from Irving R. Warner, 3235 Berry Drive, Studio City, California 91604. $17.00.

Colorado (approximately 250 foundations). *Colorado Foundation Directory 1984-85.* 4th edition. Co-sponsored by the Junior League of Denver, Inc., the Denver Foundation, and the Attorney General of Colorado. 1984. Based on 1982 and 1983 (mostly 1982) 990-PF returns filed with the IRS and information supplied by foundations; entries include statement of purpose, sample grants and officers. Also sections on proposal writing, sample proposal, and sample budget form. Available from Colorado Foundation Directory, Junior League of Denver, Inc., 6300 East Yale Avenue, Denver, Colorado 80222. Make check payable to: Colorado Foundation Directory. $10.00 prepaid.

Connecticut (61 foundations). *Directory of the Major Connecticut Foundations.* Compiled by Logos, Inc. 1982. 49 p. Based on 1979-80 990-PF and 990-AR IRS returns, foundation publications and information from the Office of the Attorney General in Hartford. Arranged alphabetically by foundation; entries include grant range, sample grants, geographic limitations, officers and directors. Index of subjects. Available from Logos, Inc., 7 Park Street, Room 212, Attleboro, Massachusetts 02703. $19.95 prepaid.

Connecticut (approximately 750 foundations). *1984 Connecticut Foundation Directory.* Edited by Michael E. Burns. 1983. 148 p. Based primarily on 1982 and 1983 990-PF returns filed with the Connecticut Attorney General. Main section arranged alphabetically by foundation; entries include complete grants list and principal officer; no statement of purpose. Index of foundations by city and alphabetical index. Available from OUA/DATA, 81 Saltonstall Avenue, New Haven, Connecticut 06513. $20 plus $1.00 postage and handling.

Connecticut (approximately 769 corporations). *Guide to Corporate Giving in Connecticut.* Edited by Michael E. Burns. 1982. 374 p. Based on information supplied by corporations. Main section arranged alphabetically by corporation; entries for most corporations include areas of interest, giving policies, geographic prefence, and contact person; some sample grants. Indexes of corporations by town. Available from OUA/DATA, 81 Saltonstall Avenue, New Haven, Connecticut 06513. $20.00 plus $1.50 postage.

Delaware (154 foundations). *Delaware Foundations.* Compiled by United Way of Delaware, Inc., 1983. x, 120 p. Based on 1979 through 1981 990-PF and 990-AR returns filed with the IRS, annual reports, and information supplied by foundations. Main section arranged alphabetically by foundation; entries include statement of purpose and officers, grant analysis, type of recipient; no sample grants. Detailed information on 111 private foundations, a list of 27 operating foundations, and a sampling of out-of-state foundations with a pattern of giving in Delaware. Two indexes; alphabetical listing of all foundations, all trustees and officers. Available from United Way of Delaware, Inc., 701 Shipley Street, Wilmington, Delaware 19801. $14.50 prepaid.

District of Columbia (approximately 500 foundations). *The Directory of Foundations of the Greater Washington Area.* Edited by Elizabeth Frazier. 1984. 125 p. Based primarily on 1982 990-PF returns filed with the IRS. Sections on large foundations, small foundations and publicly supported institutions arranged alphabetically; entries include areas of interest, officers and directors, high and low grant and five highest grants. Glossary of terms. Indexes of trustees and managers, foundations by asset size and alphabetical index of foundations. Available from the Community Foundation of Greater Washington, 3221 M Street, NW, Washington, DC 20007 or College University Research Institute, Inc., 1701 K Street, NW, Washington, DC 20006. $10.00 plus $1.50 postage.

Florida (437 foundations). *Guide to Foundations in Florida.* Compiled by the Florida Department of Community Affairs. 1983. 72 p. Based on 1981 and 1982 990-PF returns filed with the Florida Attorney General. Main section arranged alphabetically by foundation name; entries include principal officer, total net worth, grant range, total dollar amount of grants, total number of grants and purpose of foundation; no sample grants. Alphabetical and geographic indexes. Available from Florida Department of Community Affairs, Bureau of Local Government Assistance, Tallahassee, Florida 32301. Free.

Florida (780 foundations). *Foundation Profiles of the Southeast: Florida.* Compiled by James H. Taylor and John L. Wilson. 1983. vi, 130+ p. Based on 1978 and 1979 990-PF and 990-AR returns filed with the IRS. Main section arranged alphabetically by foundation name; entries include principal officer, assets, total grants and sample grants. No indexes. Available from James H. Taylor Associates, Inc., 804 Main Street, Williamsburg, Kentucky 40769. $39.95 prepaid.

Georgia (approximately 550 foundations). *Georgia Foundation Directory.* Compiled by Ann Bush. 1979. 28 p. Based on 1976 through 1978 990-PF and 990-AR returns filed with the IRS. Contains three sections: I. Alphabetical listing by foundation name; II. City listing by foundation name; III.

Subject listing by foundation name. Entries do not include foundation address, purpose statement, sample grants, or officers. No indexes. Available from Foundation Collection, Atlanta—Fulton Public Libary, 1 Margaret Mitchell Square, Atlanta, Georgia 30303. Free.

Georgia. (457 foundations). *Foundation Profiles of the Southeast: Georgia.* Compiled by James H. Taylor and John L. Wilson. 1983. vi, 85 p. Based on 1978 and 1979 990-PF and 990-AR returns filed with the IRS. Main section arranged alphabetically by foundation name; entries include principal officer, assets, total grants and sample grants. No indexes. Available from James H. Taylor Associates, Inc., 804 Main Street, Williamsburg, Kentucky 40769. $39.95 prepaid.

Georgia (530 foundations). *Guide to Foundations in Georgia.* Compiled by the Georgia Department of Human Resources. 1978. xv, 145 p. Based on 1975 through 1977 990-PF and 990-AR returns filed with the IRS. Main section arranged alphabetically by foundation; entries include statement of purpose, sample grants and principal officer. Indexes of foundation names, cities, and program interests. Available from State Economic Opportunity Unit, Office of District Programs, Department of Human Resources, 618 Ponce de Leon Avenue, N.E., Atlanta, Georgia 30308. Free. September 1981 Addendum available from same address. Free.

Hawaii (143 foundations, 25 local service organizations, 13 church funding sources). *A Guide to Charitable Trusts and Foundations in the State of Hawaii.* 1984. 302 p. Based on 1981 and 1982 990-PF returns filed with the IRS, annual reports and contact with foundations. Main section arranged alphabetically by foundation; entries include date established, purpose and activities, type of foundations, assets, total giving, officers and directors and number of grants, if available. Sections on program planning and proposal writing, forming a tax-exempt organization, mainland foundations, national church funding sources and local service organizations. Alphabetical index. Available from Alu Like, 401 Kamakee Street, 3rd floor, Honolulu, Hawaii 96814. $25.00 ($15.00 for nonprofits).

Idaho (89 foundations). *Directory of Idaho Foundations, 1984.* Prepared by the Caldwell Public Library. 1984. 23 p. Based on 1982 or 1983 990-PF returns filed with the IRS and questionnaires. Main section arranged alphabetically by foundation; entries include area of interest, sample grants, directors and trustees, and application deadlines. Indexed by subject and foundation name. Appendixes of inactive foundations, foundations with designated recipients and national foundations with a history of Idaho giving. Available from Caldwell Public Library, 1010 Dearborn, Caldwell, Idaho 83605. $3.00 prepaid.

Illinois (approximately 200 corporations). *The Chicago Corporate Connection: A Directory of Chicago Area Corporate Contributors, Including Downstate Illinois and Nothern Indiana.* 2nd edition. Edited by Susan M. Levy. 1983. xiii, 213 p. Based on information supplied by corporations. Main section arranged alphabetically by corporation; entries include principal business activity, local subsidiaries, giving policies, geographic preference, availability of printed materials, matching gift information, and contact person; no sample grants. Also section on guidelines for seeking corporate funding and a bibliography. Indexes of geographic locations, fields of business and matching gifts. Available from Donors Forum of Chicago, 208 South LaSalle, Chicago, Illinois 60604. $13.50 plus $1.50 postage and handling, prepaid.

Illinois (approximately 103 grantmakers). *Donors Forum Members Grants List 1982.* Edited by Susan M. Levy. 1983. xii, 253 p. A collection of grants of $500 or more awarded by Donors Forum members to organizations within the Chicago Metropolitan Area. Grantmakers arranged alphabetically under ten subject categories; entries include name of donee, amount of grant and whether the grant is new or a renewal of a previous grant; no address, financial data or officers. Appendix of miscellaneous grants. Available from Donors Forum of Chicago, 208 South LaSalle, Chicago, Illinois 60604. $20 plus $1.50 postage and handling.

Illinois (approximately 1900 foundations). *Illinois Foundation Directory.* Edited by Beatrice J. Capriotti and Frank J. Capriotti III. 1978. ix, 527 + p. Based on mostly 1976 and 1977 990-PF and 990-AR returns filed with the IRS plus correspondence with some foundations. Main section arranged alphabetically by foundation; entries include statement of purpose, sample grants and officers. Table of contents alphabetical by foundation name; no indexes. Available from the Foundation Data Center, Kenmar Center, 401 Kenmar Circle, Minnetonka, Minnesota 55343. $425 (includes seminar). Update service by annual subscription. $200.

Indiana (265 foundations). *Indiana Foundations: A Directory.* 2nd edition. Edited by Paula Reading Spear. 1981. iii, 147 p. Based on 1979 through 1980 (mostly 1980) 990-PF and 990-AR returns filed with the IRS and information supplied by foundations. Main section arranged alphabetically by foundation; entries include officers, areas of interest, sample grants, and contact person. Indexes of financial criteria, subjects, and counties. Appendixes of restricted foundations, corporate foundations, foundations for students assistance only, and dissolved foundations. Available from Central Research Systems, 320 North Meridian, Suite 515, Indianapolis, Indiana 46204. $19.95 prepaid.

Iowa (247 foundations). *Iowa Directory of Foundations.* Compiled by Daniel H. Holm. 1984. iv, 108 p. Based on returns filed with the IRS and information supplied by foundations; date of information is 1982 in most cases, no date is given in other entries. Main section arranged alphabetically by foundation; most entries include address, telephone number, Employer Identification Number, total assets, total grants, purpose and activities, officers and trustees, and contact person. Appendix of cancelled foundations. Index by city. Available from Trumpet Associates, Inc., P.O. Box 172, Dubuque, Iowa 52001. $19.75 plus $2 postage and handling.

Kansas (approximately 255 foundations). *Directory of Kansas Foundations.* Edited by Connie Townsley. 1979. 128 p. Based on 990-PF and 990-AR returns filed with the IRS. Fiscal date of information not provided. Main section arranged alphabetically by foundation; entries include areas of interest, sample arts grants and officers. Index of cities. Available from Association of Community Arts Agencies of Kansas, P.O. Box 62, Oberlin, Kansas 67749. $5.80 prepaid.

Kentucky (117 foundations). *Foundation Profiles of the Southeast: Kentucky.* Compiled by James H. Taylor and John L. Wilson. 1981. vi, 153 p. Based on 1978 and 1979 990-PF and 990-AR IRS returns. Main section arranged alphabetically by foundation; entries include assets, total number and amount of grants, sample grants and officers. No indexes. Available from James H. Taylor Associates, Inc., 804 Main Street, Williamsburg, Kentucky 40769. $39.95 prepaid.

Kentucky (101 foundations). *A Guide to Kentucky Grantmakers.* Edited by Nancy C. Dougherty. 1982. 19 p. Based on questionnaires to foundations, 1981 990-PF and 990-AR IRS returns.Arranged alphabetically by foundation; entries include assets, total grants paid, number of grants, smallest/largest grant, primary area of interest and contact person. No indexes. Available from The Louisville Foundation, Inc., 623 West Main Street, Louisville, Kentucky 40202. $7.50 prepaid.

Louisiana (229 foundations). See **Alabama.**

Maine (74 foundations). *A Directory of Foundations in the State of Maine.* 5th edition. Compiled by the Center for Research and Advanced Study. 1983. 39 p. Based on 1981 and 1982 990-PF returns filed with the IRS. Main section arranged alphabetically by city location of foundation; entries include areas of interest, sample grants and principal officer. Also sections on basic elements in a letter of inquiry, a description of IRS information returns, a sample report to funding source, and a list of recent grants. Index of subjects. Available from Center for Research and Advanced Study, University of Southern Maine, 246 Deering Avenue, Portland, Maine 04102. $5.50 prepaid.

Maine (approximately 75 corporations). *Maine Corporate Funding Directory.* 1983. 100 p. Based on information supplied by corporations. Main section arranged alphabetically by corporation; entries include contact person and, for a few corporations, the areas of interest. May be used at the Center for Research and Advanced Study, University of Southern Maine, 246 Deering Avenue, Portland, Maine 04102.

Maine (218 corporations). *Guide to Corporate Giving in Maine.* Michael E. Burns, editor. 1984. 72+ p. Based on questionnaires and telephone interviews. Main section arranged alphabetically; entries include product, plant locations, contributions and giving interests, if available. Index of foundations by city. Available from OUA/DATA, 81 Saltonstall Avenue, New Haven, Connecticut 06513. $15.00.

Maryland (approximately 380 foundations). *1982 Annual Index Foundation Reports.* Compiled by the Office of the Attorney General. 1983. Based on 1982 990-PF returns received by the Maryland State Attorney General's Office. Main section arranged alphabetically by foundation; entries include statement of purpose and complete list of grants, and officers. Available from the Office of the Attorney General, 7 North Calvert Street, Baltimore, Maryland 21202. Attention: Sharon Sullivan. $35.00 prepaid.

Massachusetts (549+ foundations). *Massachusetts Foundation Directory.* Prepared by Associated Grantmakers of Massachusetts. 1983. 136 p. Based on 1979 through 1981 990-PF and 990-AR returns filed with the IRS, and questionnaire responses. Main section arranged alphabetically by foundation name; entries include emphasis and program areas, total grants, range, assets, trustees, contact person; no sample grants. Indexes by program areas, city; index of foundations granting support to individuals. Appendixes of smaller Massachusetts foundations, company-sponsored foundations and recently terminated foundations. Available from Associated Grantmakers of Massachusetts, Inc., 294 Washington Street, Suite 501, Boston, Massachusetts 02108. $15.00 + $2.50 handling.

Massachusetts (960 foundations). *A Directory of Foundations in the Commonwealth of Massachusetts.* Edited by John Parker Huber. 2nd edition. 1976. xii, 161 p. Based on 1974 990-PF and 990-AR returns filed with the IRS. Main section arranged alphabetically by foundation; entries include sample grants and officers; no statement of purpose. Indexes of geographical areas and largest single grants awarded. Appendixes of additions including initial returns, relocation in Massachusetts, and previously existing foundations appearing for the first time and of deletions including final returns, relocations outside of Massachusetts, and first edition foundations not included because of lack of data. Available from Eastern Connecticut State College Foundation, Inc., P.O. Box 431, Willimantic, Connecticut 06226. $15.00 prepaid. Limited quantities available.

Massachusetts (56 Boston area foundations). *Directory of the Major Greater Boston Foundations.* 1981. 48 p. Based on 1975 through 1980 990-PF and 990-AR returns filed with the IRS. Main section arranged alphabetically by foundation; entries include statement of purpose, sample grants and officers. Index of fields of interest. Available from Logos Associates, 12 Gustin, Attleboro, Massachusetts 02703. $19.95 prepaid.

Massachusetts (737 corporations). *Guide to Corporate Giving in Massachusetts.* Michael E. Burns, editor. 1983. 97 p. Based on questionnaires and telephone interviews. Main section arranged alphabetically by city and zip code; entries include product, amount given annually, frequency, area of interest and non-cash contributions. Index of corporations by city. Available from OUA/DATA, 81 Saltonstall Avenue, New Haven, Connecticut 06513. $30.00 plus $1.50 postage and handling.

Massachusetts (approximately 150 foundations). *Private Sector Giving: Greater Worcester Area.* Prepared by The Social Service Planning Corporation. 1983. 184 p. Based on 1978 through 1981 information from 990-PF and 990-AR forms filed with the IRS and surveys. Main section arranged alphabetically by foundation; entries include financial data, trustees and grants. Indexes of foundations and areas of subject interest. Available from The Social Service Planning Corporation, 340 Main Street, Suite 329, Worcester, Massachusetts 01608. $25.00 plus $2.25 postage and handling.

Michigan (859 foundations). *The Michigan Foundation Directory.* 4th edition. Prepared by the Council of Michigan Foundations and Michigan League for Human Services. 1983. vii, 154 p. Based on information compiled from foundations, The Foundation Center, and primarily 1981-1982 990-PF returns filed with the IRS. Main section arranged in four parts: Section I is mainly an alphabetical listing of 335 Michigan foundations having assets of $200,000 or making annual grants of at least $25,000 with entries including statement of purpose and officers, geographic priority, limitations, application procedures, but no sample grants; Section I also provides brief information on 460 foundations making grants of less than $25,000 annually, geographical listing of foundations by city, terminated foundations and special purpose foundations; Section II is a listing of 48 corporate giving programs and corporate foundations; Section III is a survey of Michigan foundation philanthropy; and Section IV provides information on seeking grants. Indexes of subject/areas of interest; donors, trustees, officers; and foundation names. Available from Michigan League for Human Services, 300 North Washington Square, Suite 311, Lansing, Michigan 48893. $15.00 prepaid.

Minnesota (420+ grantmakers). *Guide to Minnesota Foundations and Corporate Giving Programs.* Prepared by the Minnesota Council on Foundations. 1983. xxiv, 149 p. Based primarily on 1981 and 1982 IRS 990-PF returns and a survey of grantmakers. Main section arranged alphabetically by foundation name; entries include program interests, officers and directors, assets, total grants, number of grants, range, and sample grants. Some entries include geographic orientation, types of organizations funded and types of support. Indexes of foundations, types of organizations funded by specific grantmakers, and grantmakers by size. Appendixes of inactive foundations, foundations with designated recipients, foundations making grants only outside of Minnesota and foundations not accepting applications. Also section on funding research in Minnesota. Available from University of Minnesota Press, 2037 University Avenue S.E., Minneapolis, Minnesota 55414. $14.95 plus 6% sales tax or tax exempt number for Minnesota residents.

Minnesota (598 foundations). *Minnesota Foundation Directory.* Edited by Beatrice J. Capriotti and Frank J. Capriotti III. 1976. 274+ p. Based on 1973 and 1974 990-PF and 990-AR returns filed with the IRS. Main section arranged alphabetically by foundation; entries include statement of purpose, sample grants and officers.Indexes of donors, administrators and trustees, and banks and trust companies as corporate trustees. Available from Foundation Data Center, Ridgedale State Bank Building, 1730 South Plymouth Road, Suite 202, Minnetonka, Minnesota 55343. $275. (Includes seminar and research training seminar.) Update service by annual subscription. $180.

Mississippi (54 foundations). See **Alabama.**

Montana (50 Montana and 20 Wyoming foundations). *The Montana and Wyoming Foundations Directory.* Compiled by Paula Deigert, Jane Kavanaugh, and Ellen Alweis. 2nd edition. 1983. 23 p. Based on 990-PF and 990-AR returns filed with the IRS, the National Data Book, and information supplied by foundations. Main section arranged alphabetically by foundation; entries include areas of interest and contact person; no sample grants. Indexes of foundation names and areas of interest. Available from Grant Assistance, Eastern Montana College Library, 1500 North 30th Street, Billings, Montana 59101. $6.00 prepaid.

Nebraska (approximately 154 foundations). *Nebraska Foundation Directory.* Compiled by the Junior League of Omaha. 1981. 14 p. Based on mostly 1979 and 1980 990-PF and 990-AR returns filed with the IRS. Main section arranged alphabetically by foundation; entries include statement of purpose and officers. No sample grants or indexes. Available from Junior League of Omaha, 808 South 74th Plaza, Omaha, Nebraska 68114. $3.00.

Nevada (41 foundations). *Nevada Foundation Directory.* Prepared by Vlasta Honsa and Annetta Yousef. 1985. 64 p. Based on 1982 and 1983 990-PF forms filed with the IRS and interviews with foundations. Main section arranged alphabetically by foundation; entries include contact person, financial data, funding interests and sample grants. Section on inactive and defunct Nevada foundations. Section on 30 national foundations that fund Nevada projects. Index of fields of interest and index of foundation location. Available from: Community Relations Department, Clark County Library District, 1401 East Flamingo Road, Las Vegas, Nevada 89109.

New Hampshire (approximately 400 foundations). *Directory of Charitable Funds in New Hampshire.* 3rd edition. June 1976. 107 p. Based on 1974 and 1975 records in the New Hampshire Attorney General's Office. Updated with cumulative, annual supplement published in June. Main section arranged alphabetically by foundation; entries include statement of purpose and officers; no sample grants. Indexes of geographical areas when restricted, and of purpose when not geographically restricted. Available from the Office of the Attorney General, Charitable Trust, State House Annex, Concord, New Hampshire 03301. $2.00. Annual supplement, which includes changes, deletions, and additions, available from the same address for $2.00 prepaid. Make check payable to "State of N.H."

New Jersey (approximately 400 foundations and approximately 600 corporations). *The New Jersey Mitchell Guide: Foundations, Corporations, and Their Managers.* Edited by Janet A. Mitchell. 1983. xiii, 383 p. Based on 1980 and 1981 990-PF and 990-AR returns filed with the IRS and information supplied by foundations. Main section arranged alphabetically by foundation; entries include sample grants and officers; no statement of purpose. Also sections on corporations. Indexes of foundations and corporations by county and by managers. Appendixes of foundation statistics, foundations with assets over $1 million, and foundations with grant totals over $100,000. Available from The Mitchell Guide, P.O. Box 413, Princeton, New Jersey 08542. $35.00 prepaid.

New Jersey (approximately 66 foundations). *The Directory of the Major New Jersey Foundations.* First edition. Prepared by Logos Associates. 1983. 56 p. Based on 1980 through 1982 financial information. Arranged alphabetically by foundation; entries include contact person, activities, officers and directors, geographic limitations, financial data, and sample grants. No indexes. Available from Logos Associates, Room 212, 7 Park Street, Attleboro, Massachusetts 02703. $19.95.

New Mexico (approximately 41 foundations). *New Mexico Private Foundations Directory.* Edited by Willaim G. Murrell, and William M. Miller. 1982. 77 p. Main section arranged alphabetically by foundation; entries include contact person, program purpose, areas of interest, financial data, application procedure, meeting times and publications. Also sections on proposal writing, private and corporate grantmanship and bibliography. No indexes. Available from New Moon Consultants, P.O. Box 532, Tijeras,

New Mexico 87059. $5.50 plus $1.00 postage. New edition available mid-1984.

New York (approximately 140 organizations). *Guide to Grantmakers: Rochester Area.* 2nd edition. Compiled by the Monroe County Library System. 1983. vii, 220 p. Based on contact with organizations and 1980 through 1982 (mostly 1981) 990-PF and 990-AR returns filed with the IRS. Main section arranged alphabetically by organization, including foundations, corporations, associations, nonprofit organizations offering funds, services or products; entries include statement of purpose and officers; no sample grants. Also a section on liquidated and relocated foundations. Index of fields of interest. Appendixes of glossary of terms and bibliography. Published by Urban Information Center, Monroe County Library System. Order from the Urban Information Center, Monroe County Library System, 115 South Avenue, Rochester, New York, 14604. $14.00 prepaid. May be used in libraries of Monroe County Library System.

New York (62 foundations and 125 corporation). *The Mitchell Guide to Foundations, Corporations and Their Managers: Central New York State* (includes Binghamton, Corning, Elmira, Geneva, Ithaca, Oswego, Syracuse and Utica). Edited by Rowland L. Mitchell. 1984. Based on 990-PF returns filed with the IRS. Main sections arranged alphabetically by foundation and by corporation; entries include managers, financial data, and sample grants. Alphabetical indexes of foundations and corporations and index to managers. Available from The Mitchell Guide, P.O. Box 413, Princeton, New Jersey 08542. $25.00 prepaid.

New York (149 foundations and 125 corporations). *The Mitchell Guide to Foundations, Corporations and Their Managers: Long Island* (includes Nassau and Suffolk Counties). Edited by Rowland L. Mitchell. 1984. Based on 990-PF returns filed with the IRS. Main sections arranged alphabetically by foundation and by corporation; entries include managers, financial data, and sample grants. Alphabetical indexes of foundations and corporations and index to managers. Available from The Mitchell Guide, P.O. Box 413, Princeton, New Jersey 08542. $30.00 prepaid.

New York (61 foundations and 125 corporations). *The Mitchell Guide to Foundations, Corporations and Their Managers: Upper Hudson Valley* (includes the Capital Area, Glenn Flass, Newburgh, Plattsburgh, Poughkeepsie and Schenectady). Edited by Rowland L. Mitchell. 1984. Based on 990-PF returns filed with the IRS. Main sections arranged alphabetically by foundation and by corporation; entries include managers, financial data, and sample grants. Alphabetical indexes of foundations and corporations and index to managers. Available from The Mitchell Guide, P.O. Box 413, Princeton, New Jersey 08542. $25.00 prepaid.

New York (148 foundations and 58 corporations). *The Mitchell Guide to Foundations, Corporations and Their Managers: Westchester* (includes Putnam, Rockland and parts of Orange Counties). Edited by Rowland L. Mitchell. 1984. Based on 990-PF returns filed with the IRS. Main sections arranged alphabetically by foundation and by corporation; entries include managers, financial data, and sample grants. Alphabetical indexes of foundations and corporations and index to managers. Available from The Mitchell Guide, P.O. Box 413, Princeton, New Jersey 08542. $30.00 prepaid.

New York (125 foundations and 132 corporations). *The Mitchell Guide to Foundations, Corporations and Their Managers: Western New York State* (includes Buffalo, Jamestown, Niagara Falls and Rochester). Edited by Rowland L. Mitchell. 1984. Based on 990-PF returns filed with the IRS. Main sections arranged alphabetically by foundation and by corporation; entries include managers, financial data, and sample grants. Alphabetical indexes of foundations and corporations and index to managers. Available from The Mitchell Guide, P.O. Box 413, Princeton, New Jersey 08542. $30.00 prepaid.

New York (1,832 foundations and 750 corporations). *The New York City Mitchell Guide: Foundations, Corporations, and Their Managers.* Edited by Rowland L. Mitchell. 1983. xi, 413 p. Based on 1980 through 1982 990-PF and 990-AR returns filed with the IRS. Main sections arranged alphabetically by foundation and by corporation; foundation entries include managers, financial data, and sample grants; no statement of purpose. Alphabetical indexes of foundations and corporations. Available from The Mitchell Guide, P.O. Box 413, Princeton, New Jersey 08542. $75.00 prepaid.

North Carolina (492 foundations). *Foundation Profiles of the Southeast: North Carolina, South Carolina.* Compiled by James H. Taylor and John L. Wilson. 1983. vi, 100+ p. Based on 1978 and 1979 990-PF and 990-AR returns. Main sections arranged alphabetically by foundation name; entries include principal officer, assets, total grants and sample grants. No indexes. Available from James H. Taylor Associates, Inc., 804 Main Street, Williamsburg, Kentucky 40769. $39.95 prepaid.

Ohio (1800 foundations). *Charitable Foundations Directory of Ohio.* 5th edition. 1982. 101 p. Based on 1977 through 1982 records in the Ohio Attorney General's Office and returns filed with the IRS. Main section arranged alphabetically by foundation; entries include statement of purpose and contact person; no sample grants. Indexes of foundation by county location and purpose. Available from Charitable Foundations Directory, Attorney General's Office, 30 East Broad Street, 15th floor, Columbus, Ohio 43215. $6.00 prepaid.

Ohio (38 foundations). *Guide to Charitable Foundations in the Greater Akron Area.* 2nd edition. Prepared by Grants Department. 1981. 48 p. Based on United Way files, the Charitable Foundations Directory of Ohio, 990-PF and 990-AR returns filed with the IRS, and information supplied by foundations. Main section arranged alphabetically by foundation; entries include statement of purpose, sample grants, and officers. Also section proposal writing. Appendixes include indexes of assets, grants, and officers and trustees. Available from Grants Department, United Way of Summit County, P.O. Box 1260, 90 North Prospect Street, Akron, Ohio 44304. $7.50.

Ohio (22 foundations). *Directory of Dayton Area Grantmakers.* 1983 edition. Prepared by Carol Richardson and Judy Tye. 1983. xii, 29 p. Based on 1980 through 1982 data. Main section arranged alphabetically by foundation; most entries include contact person, fields of interest and limitations, and total assets, total and number of grants. Section on 'Applying for a Grant' and glossary of grantmakers terms. Alphabetical index and index of interests. Available from Belinda Hogue, 449 Patterson Road, Apt. A, Dayton, Ohio 45419. Free plus $1.25 postage and handling.

Oklahoma (approximately 150 foundations). *Directory of Oklahoma Foundations.* 2nd edition. Edited by Thomas E. Broce. 1982. 284 p. Based on data from cooperating foundations or from 1974 through 1981 990-PF and 990-AR returns filed with the IRS. Main sections arranged alphabetically by foundation; entries include statement of purpose and officers for some foundations; no sample grants. Index of foundation and grant activities. Available from University of Oklahoma Press, 1005 Asp Avenue, Norman, Oklahoma 73019. $22.50 plus $.86 postage.

Oregon (approximately 300 foundations). *The Guide to Oregon Foundations.* 3rd edition. Produced by the United Way of the Columbia-Willamette. 1984. xv, 208 p. Based on 990-PF and CT-12 forms filed with the Oregon Register of Charitable Trusts and information supplied by foundations. Main section arranged alphabetically by foundation within six subdivisions: general purpose foundations, special purpose foundations, student aid or scholarship funds, service clubs, decicated purpose and national foundations with an active interest in Oregon; entries include statement of purpose, officers, assets, total grants, sample grants and application information. Appendixes include Oregon foundations having assets of $500,000 or more, terminated foundations, inactive foundations, new foundations, regional breakdown of foundations and national foundation grants to Oregon. Index of foundation names. Available from Bonnie Smith, the United Way of the Columbia-Willamette, 718 West Burnside, Portland, Oregon 97209. $15.00 plus $.50 postage.

Pennsylvania (2267 foundations). *Directory of Pennsylvania Foundations.* 2nd edition. Compiled by S. Damon Kletzien, editor, with assistance from Margaret H. Chalfant and Frances C. Ritchey. 1981. xv, 280 p. Based on 1979 and 1980 990-PF and 990-AR returns filed with the IRS and information supplied by foundations. Main section arranged alphabetically within geographic regions; profile entries include statement of purpose, grants of $100 or larger, application guidelines, and officers of 914 foundations meeting criteria of assets exceeding $75,000 or awarding grants totaling $4,000 or more; for foundations under criteria, entries include foundation name, address and status code only. Appendixes on approaching foundations, program planning and proposal writing, and broadening the foundation search. Indexes of officers, directors and trustees; major interests; and foundation names. Available from Directory of Pennsylvania Foundations, c/o Friends of the Free Library, Logan Square at 19th Street, Philadelphia, Pennsylvania 19103. Make check payable to: Friends of the Free Library of Philadelphia. $18.50 plus $1.11 for PA sales tax if applicable.

Rhode Island (91 foundations). *Directory of Grant-Making Foundations in Rhode Island.* Compiled by the Council for Community Services. 1983. 47 p. Based on 1980 and 1981 990-PF and 990-AR returns filed with the IRS, information from the Rhode Island Attorney General's Office and information from foundations. Main section arranged alphabetically by foundation; entries include officers and trustees, assets, total dollar amount of grants and total number of grants, statement of purpose, geographic restrictions, application information and sample grants. Includes "Introduction to Foundations"; indexes of foundations by total dollar amount of grants made, foundations by location and by area of interest. Available from the Council for Community Services, 229 Waterman Street, Providence, Rhode Island 02906. $8.00 prepaid.

Rhode Island (188 corporations). *Guide to Corporate Giving in Rhode Island.* Michael E. Burns, editor. 1984. 58 p. Based on questionnaires and telephone interviews. Main section arranged alphabetically; entries include product, plant location, giving interests and non-cash giving, where available. Index of corporations by city. Available from OUA/DATA, 81 Saltonstall Avenue, New Haven, Connecticut 06513. $15.00.

South Carolina (174 foundations). *South Carolina Foundation Directory.* 2nd edition. Edited by Anne K. Middleton. 1983. 51 p. Based on 1981 and 1982 990-PF returns filed with the IRS. Main section arranged alphabetically by foundation; entries include areas of interest, principal officer, assets, total grants, number of grants, range and geographic limitations. Indexes of foundations by city and field of interest. Available from Anne K. Middleton, Senior Reference Librarian, South Carolina State

Library, P.O. Box 11469, Columbia, South Carolina 29211. Send $5.00 check payable to the South Carolina State Library.

South Carolina (49 foundations). See **North Carolina.**

Tennessee (83 foundations; 23 corporations). *Tennessee Directory of Foundations and Corporate Philanthropy.* Revised edition. Published by City of Memphis, Bureau of Intergovernmental Management. 1982. iv, 134 p. Based primarily on 1980 and 1981 990-PF and 990-AR returns filed with the IRS and questionnaires. Two main sections arranged alphabetically by foundation and alphabetically by corporation; entries include contact person, contact procedure, fields of interest, geographic limitations, financial data, officers and trustees and sample grants. Indexes of foundations and corporations by name, fields of interest and geographic area of giving. Appendixes of foundations giving less than $10,000 a year, and major corporations in Tennessee which employ more than 300 persons. Available from City of Memphis, Bureau of Intergovernmental Management, 125 North Mid-America Mall, Room 508, Memphis, Tennessee 38103.

Tennessee (202 foundations). See **Kentucky.**

Texas (approximately 1374 foundations). *Hooper Directory of Texas Foundations.* Compiled and edited by William J. Hooper, Jr. and Amie Rodnick. 1983. 200 p. Based on mostly 1982 990-PF returns filed with the IRS. Main section arranged alphabetically by foundation; entries include areas of interest and contact person; no sample grants. Also a section on dissolved foundations. Indexes of areas of interest, cities and trustees. Appendix of top 100 foundations. Available from Texas Foundation Research Center, P.O. Box 5494, Austin, Texas 78763. Make check payable to: TFRC. $26.50 prepaid. Add $1.25 for sales tax if applicable.

Texas (approximately 200 foundations). *The Guide to Texas Foundations.* 2nd edition. Edited by Jed Riffe. 1980. 103 p. Based on data from cooperating foundations and from 1977 and 1978 records in the Texas Attorney General's Office and Dallas Public Library. Main section arranged alphabetically by city location of foundation; entries include statement of purpose, sample grants, and officers. Covers foundations with grant totals over $30,000 per year. Indexes of foundation names and areas of interest. Available from Marianne Cline, Dallas Public Library, 1954 Commerce Street, Dallas, Texas 75201. $10.00 prepaid.

Texas (approximately 115 foundations). *Directory of Tarrant County Foundations.* Prepared by Catherine Rhodes and the Junior League of Fort Worth. 1984. 150+ p. Based on 1982 and 1983 990-PF forms filed with the IRS and foundation questionnaires. Main section arranged alphabetically by foundation; entries include financial data, background and program interest, officers and trustees, types of support and geographic focus.

Indexes of foundations, trustees and officers, types of support and fields of interest. Appendices of foundations by asset amount and foundations by total grants. Available from Funding Information Center, Texas Christian University Library, Fort Worth, Texas 76129. $6.00 plus $1.00 postage and handling.

Virginia (approximately 500 foundations). *Virginia Foundations 1984.* Published by the Grants Resource Library of Hampton, Virginia. 1984. 200+ p. Based on 1980 through 1983 990-PF and 990-AR returns filed with the IRS. Main section arranged alphabetically by foundation; entries include officers and directors, assets, total grants and sample grants. Index by foundation name. Available from Sharen Sinclair, Grants Resource Library, Hampton City Hall, 9th floor, 22 Lincoln Street, Hampton, Virginia 23669. $10.00 prepaid.

Virginia (326 foundations). See **Kentucky.**

Washington (approximately 968 organizations). *Charitable Trust Directory.* Compiled by the Office of the Attorney General. 1983. 242 p. Based on 1982 records in the Washington Attorney General's Office. Includes information on all charitable organizations and trusts reporting to Attorney General under the Washington Charitable Trust Act. Main section arranged alphabetically by organization; entries include statement of purpose and officers. No sample grants or indexes. Available from the Office of the Attorney General, Temple of Justice, Olympia, Washington 98504. $4.00 prepaid.

West Virginia (approximately 99 foundations). *West Virginia Foundation Directory.* Compiled and edited by William Seeto. 1979. 49 p. Based on 1977 and 1978 990-PF and 990-AR returns filed with the IRS. Main section arranged alphabetically by foundation; entries include sample grants and officers; no statement of purpose. Also a section on inactive or terminated foundations. Index of counties and cities. May be used at the Foundation Center collection, Kanawha County Public Library, 123 Capitol Street, Charleston, West Virginia 25301.

Wisconsin (643 foundations). *Foundations in Wisconsin: A Directory 1982.* 6th edition. Compiled by Susan H. Hopwood. 1982. xiii, 280 p. Based on 1980 and 1981 990-PF and 990-AR returns filed with the IRS. Main section arranged alphabetically by foundation; entries include areas of interest and officers; no sample grants. Also sections listing inactive foundations, terminated foundations, and operating foundations. Indexes of areas of interest, counties, and foundation managers. Available from The Foundation Collection, Marquette University Memorial Library, 1415 West Wisconsin Avenue, Milwaukee, Wisconsin 53233. $15.00 prepaid plus $.75 sales tax for Wisconsin residents, or Wisconsin tax exempt number.

Wyoming (45 foundations). *Wyoming Foundations Directory.* Prepared by Joy Riske. 1982. 2nd edition. 54 p. Based on 1980 through 1982 990-PF and 990-AR returns filed with the IRS and a survey of the foundations. Main section arranged alphabetically by foundation; entries include statement of purpose and contact person when available. Also sections on foundations based out-of-state that award grants to Wyoming and a list of foundations awarding educational loans and scholarships. Index of foundations. Available from Laramie County Community College Library, 1400 East College Drive, Cheyenne, Wyoming 82007. Free. $1.00 postage for out of state orders.

Wyoming (20 foundations). See **Montana.**

DATE DUE

NOV 11 '87			
FEB 10 '88			

DEMCO 38-297